MIND *yoga*

Don,
Peace, love +
a Big hug!
[illegible]

MIND *yoga*

MAKE YOUR MENTAL HEALTH
STRONGER
ONE THOUGHT AT A TIME

Annette Quarrier

Mind Yoga

Book design by Jessika Hazelton
Printed in the United States of America
The Troy Book Makers • Troy, New York • thetroybookmakers.com

To order additional copies of this title,
contact your favorite local bookstore
or visit www.shoptbmbooks.com

ISBN: 978-1-61468-512-8

dedication

IN LOVING MEMORY OF

Stan Valenti (4/6/50-11/17/94)

Tom Dexter (4/8/60-8/4/85)

This book is dedicated to two wonderful men whose early and sudden deaths taught me about life... the importance of LIVING everyday to the fullest. ...to appreciate each and every person in our lives... how every breath we take is priceless...and how we should never take anyone or anything for granted.

I miss you each and every single day and wish with all my heart I could talk with you again, laugh with you right now and hug you one more time. Your LIVING, gave me and hundreds of your family and friends so much joy. I am blessed for the millions of memories we shared and I am forever grateful to have had you both in my life.

AND ALSO IN LOVING MEMORY OF

Karma Quarrier (1/4/08-4/26/19)

Karma was my dog who passed away while I was writing this book. She was the perfect dog for me and she will be in my heart always. She was a Rhodesian Ridgeback; she weighed 90 lbs. and she was kind, loving and peaceful. She rarely barked. Her personality could not have fit her name any better, as she brought "Good Karma" to everyone in her presence. She was a therapy dog and she brought joy to many residents of the local nursing home we used to visit. To add another quote to many in this book "those who teach us the most about humanity aren't always human"-Donald Hicks.

Contents

forward

> *"Your strongest muscle and your worst enemy is your mind... Train it well."*
>
> – Anonymous[1]

This book is a compilation of my first year of "Mind Yoga Quick Quotes with AnnetteQ" podcasts. Throughout the year, many commented on how much they liked my podcast but they wished they had written down a point I made, a question I asked, or a quote I used. Some even suggested I write a book.

I use the term "Mind Yoga" because I believe keeping our minds healthy is just as important as keeping our bodies healthy. We spend time working out our bodies to get in shape and stay healthy but how much time do we spend getting mentally fit?

Working out our minds is usually associated with doing a crossword puzzle or playing along with the contestants on Jeopardy. Rarely, if at all, do we take time out of our day to think about our mental health. Mental health in our society usually has a negative connotation instead of a positive one. We may remark someone is in great physical health but how often have you remarked or heard someone is in great mental health?

1 Every effort was made to find the author of all quotes in this book. If a reader knows an author I have not credited, please send me an email at annetteq.com@gmail.com

Mental health begins by understanding that we have control over our thoughts. Whether you listen to my podcast, or read this book, my hope is that you start to realize you do have the option to think about circumstances from different perspectives and by so doing, you do have control over your thoughts and you can start to find peace in your life.

In my podcast, I take a quote each week and talk about it from a viewpoint you may never have thought about. I ask some questions to get you to start stretching your mind, and I encourage you to take a challenge each week based on the quote.

This book follows my first year of podcasts. Each chapter is a different quote from my weekly show, but unlike my podcast which is "quick," in this book I delve into the topic a bit more to allow for further mind stretching. Each chapter ends like my podcasts, with a challenge. The arrangement of the chapters differ from my podcasts in order to keep common themes together for easier reading. You are free to read this book any way you choose, but it has 52 chapters and can be used as a weekly guide to help you get in optimal mental health shape. As you read this book, may you realize the power you hold in being mentally fit.

chapter one

WHAT'S WORTH YOUR ENERGY?

> *"Become more aware of what's really worth your energy."*
>
> – Author Unknown

We all give off energy whether we realize it or not. Every single second of the day, our body is giving off either positive or negative energy. How can you know this is true? Think about the times you have walked into a room and you know instantly someone is in a bad mood. You haven't even said a word to them, they haven't said a word to you; but you can just tell by the energy they're giving off that they're in a bad mood. Same is true if they're in a good mood. You feel a lightness around them. Your body becomes relaxed because their energy is positive. You can just feel they are in a good mood.

We all have a choice every day, at any moment, to shift our energy; to change it from negative to positive, or visa-versa. And, we have a choice too, to look at any situation and decide whether we're going to let it drain us or give us energy. This is why the quote "Become more aware of what's really worth your energy" is something to think about more deeply. Positive energy is when we are feeling good, from the inside out. We may remark someone is "beaming"; this is an example of positive energy. Negative energy, on the other hand, is energy we emit when we are feeling bad.

Situations are constantly presented to us, and we are the only ones who can choose whether they are worth our time. If it's important to us, then we are probably going to want to give it our energy; but if it's not going to be beneficial to us, we probably don't want to give it our energy. But how do we know if we're giving our energy away and it may not be the best thing for us to do? When we get caught up in trivial little things and we find ourselves feeling defensive, is a good time to think again whether we want to give something our energy. We can often feel our body start to tense up when we're about to give off negative energy. When we have to make a point, or prove we're right; or if we are stressing something has to be done our way, as if there is no other option; is another good indication we are wasting our positive energy and using it negatively.

It is in times like this that I ask you to try and just "take a pause". Think about whether you want this situation to drain you or can you just LET IT GO? Does it really matter if you get your point across if you lose your peace in the process? Letting things go is not a weakness. In fact it takes a strong person to let things go. I'm sure there are people who would disagree with me, but letting go of what drains your energy will give you more positive energy and will make you stronger—mentally.

Think about your energy and start to notice the energy you give off. When you are in a bad mood, notice how your body feels. Is it tensing up? Do you have a tightness in your chest? Does your breath start to quicken its pace? When you are in a good mood, notice your energy. Do your muscles relax? Do you feel calmer? Start to notice other people's energy too. If you notice someone in a bad mood, step away from their energy if you can. And, when you do, notice if your energy shifts at all too; maybe you are suddenly more relaxed by moving yourself away from their energy.

Now, think about what's really worth your energy. At the end of this chapter there is space for you to write down what you believe is worth your energy. Make a commitment to put your energy into these things. And, if something is not on this list, think again whether you want to give it your energy—and if so, for how long. I've given you space to list things not worth your energy too, because once you decide they aren't worth your energy, you need to stop giving them your energy. These lists will help remind you what is important to you and what's not.

"Become more aware of what's really worth your energy" and remember it's up to you to monitor what you spend your energy on. Are you going to spend it on something that energizes you or drains you? The choice is yours to make!

CHALLENGE

Start to notice when something
is not worth your energy
and don't give it your energy.
Walk away, don't respond, don't waste your energy.

Things Worth My Energy:

____

____

____

____

____

____

____

Things Not Worth My Energy:

chapter two

POSSIBLE OR (I'M)POSSIBLE?

Alice in Wonderland: *"This is impossible."*
The Mad Hatter: *"Only if you believe it is."*

- Lewis Carroll

"Nothing is impossible,
the word itself says 'I'm Possible'!"

- Audrey Hepburn

As adults we learn the fairy tales we watched as children were more than just a funny form of entertainment. We now know and understand most cartoons have hidden meanings and messages, sprinkled with adult humor, and they are often even more entertaining to watch as adults than when we were younger. And we've learned in most cartoons, there's a lesson to be learned. The lesson is usually about the power in believing in ourselves.

This first quote above is from Alice in Wonderland and points out the obvious, that what we believe is very often what will happen in our life. The Mad Hatter was a very wise character who knew the enormous power of believing in yourself. He knew what we believe is often what we receive. We are at times our own worse enemy. We self sabotage ourselves the minute we say something is impossible. When we think or say something is impossible, we set ourselves up for defeat before we even try.

And when we take a look at the second quote by Audrey Hepburn, "Nothing is Impossible, the word itself says 'I'm Possible'!" we are looking at a negative word from a different perspective. I love that. I love how the letters in words can have double meanings by making the word into two or even three words. Another one I like is Healthy Self and Heal Thy Self. How many words can we do this with? Not many is my guess, but let's stop and think about these two quotes and how often we set ourselves up for defeat in our minds, before we even try something. Have you ever talked yourself out of something you wanted to do, by making a mental list in your head of why it's not a good idea? Do you ever utter "this won't work" before you even try it?

The way we think about things in our mind determines the trajectory of our life. The "Self Coaching Model"[2] teaches how our thoughts create our feelings, which create our actions and ultimately our results. If we think something we want is impossible, we may not even try to make it happen. And, if we do try it, we may do it half heartedly, because in the back of our mind, we've already accepted defeat. Why? Because if we think what we want is impossible for us to have, we will feel a number of negative emotions and we won't be able to get motivated. Our thoughts will make us demotivated and our action may be no action. Our result will then prove our thought. Our results always goes back to our thoughts. In

2 This model I learned during my Life Coach Training through the Martha Beck Institute, and is a model Brooke Castillo developed further and I learned more about while a student of hers.

this case, the reason it will be impossible is because we think it is. It's important to understand our thought will determine our result every time.

But there is good news—we can change the trajectory of our lives. We really can, we just have to believe we can. We have to listen to the Mad Hatter and not Alice in Wonderland. We have to remember Audrey Hepburn's statement "I'm Possible". Once we truly believe that nothing is impossible, we can then start to feel empowered and we can start to take action.

Here's another question to ponder...do you ever use the words "I can't"? These two words used together are in my opinion two of the most negative and dangerous words in the human vocabulary. They give us a justification for not trying, for not believing in ourselves. What would probably be more truthful is to simply comment "I won't" but we avoid saying this because the words have a much stronger negative connotation and sounds juvenile. It's so easy to remark "I can't"; it relieves us of any responsibility. When we hear "I can't" we assume the person saying them has a reason why they can't. We may even feel compassion for them. If we hear "I won't" we assume they are being obstinate.

The next time you catch yourself about to use the words "I can't" think about whether you really "can't". Maybe you "CAN" but you're so accustomed to using the words "I can't" they come out of your mouth before you even think about if you can. What's keeping you from "I can"? Is it because you think it's impossible for you to do? Think again, the Mad Hatter was right after all... "only if you believe it is". You CAN make the impossible, possible. It's your decision what you want to believe. Believing you CAN may seem impossible, but believing you can't will never make anything possible.

CHALLENGE

The next time you are about to use "I can't"
as your excuse, stop and think whether you can.
Do you really want to but you don't believe you can?
Or, are you using the words "I can't" instead of "I won't"?
Do you believe nothing is "Impossible"?
If what you want seems "Impossible"
remember: "I'm Possible".

What do you think is impossible for you to achieve and why? Use the following space to write down your thoughts.

chapter three

SOMEDAY

"There are seven days in the week and someday isn't one of them."

- Benny Lewis

The first time I saw this quote I laughed. It is humorous. But there is also a truth in it that isn't funny. How often do you think or even say out loud "Someday I'm going to..." When was the last time you said this? Maybe it was in reference to a trip you want to take in the future. Perhaps you're saving money to go, planning your vacation time at work, and/or figuring out when the best time for you to go would be. I don't think using "someday" in this context is what this quote is about. I believe the author was talking about the times when we use "someday" as an excuse to put off doing what we need or know we should be doing now.

We often put things off out of habit. We know we have to or we want to do something, but yet we hold off doing it. I believe if we delve down deeper we would find we use the word "Someday" when we truly aren't committed to doing something. We may want to, but there is a big difference between wanting something and actually taking action to make it happen. It could be cleaning out a closet, or the garage. We tell ourselves "Someday I'm going to clean that closet" or "Someday I'm going to clean out the garage". But until we start to actually do it, we're just putting it off. We probably have cleaned a dozen other things instead of them in the meantime, we've just spent the time it would take to clean them on other priorities.

When we're not committed to doing something, it's ok. But think about why you can't admit you're not committed to doing it. Are you afraid of being judged? Are you afraid you'll start it and then give up because it's too much work? What is it that keeps you from making "Someday" happen today? Why don't we want to do it? What will happen if we don't do it? Why do we keep items on our "Someday" list we know are never going to get done?

And, speaking of a "Someday" list, what's on your ultimate "Someday" list? Jot a few things down below. What do you want to do "Someday"? Go ahead and list a few:

____

____

____

____

____

____

____

____

____

____

____

____

____

Now that you have a few things to refer to, how committed are you to making these things happen? What do you need to do to make these happen?

In order for anything to happen we need to take action. Stating you will do it "someday" is not taking action. It's actually inferring the action you are going to take is in the future and at an unspecified time. It's an excuse to not take action now. Someday is procrastination. Even if what we want is intended to happen in the future, we still need to take action now. When we take a vacation we don't go to the airport, buy our ticket and leave that same day. We plan ahead of time; we buy our ticket months in advance, we book our hotel, our rental car, and our reservations for various activities we are going to enjoy on our trip months in advance too.

So look at what you wrote again and decide what actions you can start now to make your "Someday" list happen. Pick one item and one action to take this week, Then you will be on your way to making it happen. And here's the best news, you don't have to figure out all the details in order to move forward. Waiting until all the details are figured out is a way of allowing yourself even more time to not take action. It's ok you haven't got it all figured out. Take baby steps if you need to, but start taking some steps. Think of it as progress, not perfection. If you wait until you have it all figured out perfectly you'll be using"someday" until you have no more days left. It's another excuse to wait. Don't get caught up in this trap. It's just that, a trap; and traps are never fun and they lead us nowhere.

We accomplish what we want to accomplish when we commit to making it happen. And, one thing is for sure, it is guaranteed to be accomplished on either a Monday, Tuesday, Wednesday, Thursday, Friday, Saturday or on a Sunday. Nothing is ever accomplished "Someday" and for that reason we should stop using the word as if it is a day of the week.

It's not. It's what procrastinators say when they want time to procrastinate more. Don't use "Someday" as your eighth day of the week. Use it as a guide to tell you what you really want and then decide the steps you are going to take and what day of the week you are going to make it happen.

CHALLENGE

Look at what's on your "Someday" list.
Take 2 items from this list and write out
the next step needed to make it happen.
Give yourself one week or less to take the next step.
Keep it going till all items are checked off your list!

Use the following space to write down the next steps for two items from your list.

Item One:

___

___

___

___

___

___

___

___

___

___

___

___

Item two:

chapter four

A USEFUL TO DO LIST

1. *Count your blessings*
2. *Practice kindness*
3. *Let go of what you can't control*
4. *Be productive (but calm)*
5. *Just breathe*

Do you ever make a "to do" list? What would happen if we incorporated the one above into our lives on a daily basis? All of the items on this list are available to everyone. There's no financial or educational requirement needed. They are free and the benefits of practicing them are priceless. We can easily check these off at the end of our day and what might be the result? Would we be happier? Would we feel more peaceful? Let's look at each one and you can decide if the benefits outweigh the effort.

*1. **Count your Blessings*** — How often do you stop and think about how blessed you are? How often do you actually Count your Blessings? If you only do it for today, I encourage you to write down five things you are grateful for. Maybe you do this already, and maybe you don't. If you don't, take a few minutes today and just try it. You don't have to write down any major, earth shattering things. They can be as simple as a bed to sleep in each night or indoor plumbing. The point is to just do it. And, if you want to make this a daily habit, go ahead. It will enrich your life in ways you can't even imagine but try it for today, just for a start.

2. Practice Kindness — A simple thing to do but I'm not sure how many of us practice this much, is just for today try to be nice to everyone you encounter. If you want to make a sarcastic remark, hold it in. If someone is trying to get into your lane on the road, let them. Tomorrow you can cut them off—I'm just kidding—but seriously for today, try to be kind to everyone, even if you are in a bad mood. Practicing kindness may even make you feel better. I have a hunch it won't ever make you feel worse. When we are kind to others we usually receive kindness in return. We get what we give. Kindness is not overrated. The benefits of practicing kindness go beyond just you and the person you are kind to. When you are kind to someone, it may prompt them to also be kind. It can start a kindness chain that is invisible but can be felt by others you don't even know. There's no downside to being kind. Practice it as much as you can. I remember once remarking to my Dad "you know Dad, you get more bees with honey than you do with vinegar" and he looked at me dumbfounded and said he never thought about that. He came from a mindset that if you want something you ask for it, you don't need to sugarcoat it. It's just the way he grew up; it wasn't in his nature to be soft spoken or to deliberately think about how you may ask a waiter for more water, or anything like that. If we were at a restaurant and he needed more water he may remark to the waiter "you know I need more water here"; almost insinuating the waiter wasn't doing his job because his water was empty. I used to cringe when he did this. I felt bad for whoever was waiting on us. My Dad was a kind man but his tone at times was not what others may interpret as kind. I use this example so you can see how we can use kindness in the smallest of circumstances. If he simply asked "Can I please have more water?" it would have sounded much kinder. We all are short and abrupt at times. Let's start noticing when we are and work on being more kind.

3. Let Go of What You Can't Control — This is my favorite item on this list and it's something I struggle with daily and have to remind myself to do. I even have a sign in my office to remind me of this, it reads "Control the Controllable's". And guess what and who you can control? Only YOU. That's right, the only person we can control is ourselves. Don't waste your time trying to control others, it's just that, a waste of time. I explore this topic more in another chapter but for now stop trying to control anything but yourself. I know it's easier said than done. Start with just one day. For one day try to make a conscious effort to Let Go of What You Can't Control. Other people will and can do whatever they want to do. Let them be who they are and you be who you are. I don't care if you're a control freak. If you are, for one day recognize when you want to control something and Let it Go.

4. Be Productive (but Calm) — So there are days when we're more productive than others. It's just a fact. Some days you get more done than other days. But I've noticed something about the days I get more done versus the days I don't; something that I've learned and helps me be more productive. What I noticed is the days I don't get freaked out over life not going as planned, I get more done. If you went back and looked at days you were more productive, you too would notice it's probably the days you were calm you got more done. And it makes perfect sense. How can we get more done if we don't remain calm? If you are calm it is usually because you have confidence that everything is going according to plan and this will always make us more productive.

5. Just Breathe — A simple process but how often do we actually stop and do this? Breath work in yoga is very important and it's also important to everyday living. When we stop to take a deep breath, we are allowing ourselves to reconnect to our soul. We are calming our nervous system down. So when you find yourself hurrying around trying to get everything you need to get done, or when something unexpected happens and it throws you off kilter—stop for a second and Just Breathe. Take a pause before you respond. I guarantee you the extra 5-10 seconds you take to inhale and exhale slowly, will not ruin your day. In yoga if you have a good instructor she will cue you when you should be breathing. We need to be our own instructor and know when to cue ourselves to take a breath. Be in touch with your body and when you feel yourself getting anxious, when your breath starts to quicken its pace, know that is a good time to stop and regulate it. Take a slow inhale and a slow exhale and just breathe a few paces this way. The airplane attendant tells us to put our oxygen mask on first before attending to anyone else. There's a reason for this. We cannot help anyone else if we don't have oxygen ourselves. So if you find yourself scrambling around and your excuse for not stopping and taking a breath is you need to help someone else, think again. You need to put the oxygen mask on yourself first. Pause and take a breath. Inhale slowly, exhale slowly. You are now ready to proceed. Remember: Just Breathe.

CHALLENGE

Incorporate a few of these items into your daily routine. Once you do, notice if you feel better.

Use the following space to make your own beneficial "to do" list. What do you want to include in your daily routine?

chapter five

BEING A VICTIM

"Do you believe you're a victim
of a great compromise,
'Cause I believe you could
change your mind, and change our lives."

- Song performed by John Mellencamp

(written by: George Green, George Michael Green, John Mellencamp)

Let's start to stretch our minds and think about this quote. I don't mean to ask the obvious, but "Do you believe you're a victim of a great compromise"? Do you get discouraged because you think everyone else's life is so much better than yours? Do you play the victim role at times? Do you often feel everyone and everything is against you? Welcome to being human—we probably all can relate to feeling this way at some point in our lives. I used to feel this way a lot of the time. No matter how hard I tried at something or even when I did accomplish something, I always felt I got the short end of the stick. I thought I struggled more than my friends and family and I didn't think that was fair at all.

I wasn't happy with me but instead of looking inward, I blamed everyone and everything else. I played the perfect "victim" role. I probably could have won an Emmy for it.

But then I started to really work on me, on my well being. I delved into self help books and I was fascinated by what I was reading about and learning. I began to understand that we are responsible for our own lives, not others. This concept is the first big hurdle we have to come to terms with if we no longer want to star as the victim in our life story. I realized that I needed to take responsibility and take control of my life. I suddenly understood that I could stop being a victim and start being the heroine in my own life. I did this by changing my mindset.

Now just to be sure you understand this concept—my life didn't change overnight. Changing your mindset is not a quick flip of the switch type thing to do. It takes time, patience and practice. Our minds want to be efficient and they prefer to run on autopilot therefore anything that is new for it to learn, takes conditioning, and conditioning takes time. Your mind will resist doing this—it will want to go back to being the victim. That's what it is used to doing and our minds are lazy. It's going to throw all sorts of ideas in your head to confirm you are the victim. It doesn't want you to change, it's "happy" with the way you are. All this mindfulness is for the birds it will tell you. Mind Yoga—you got to be kidding me it will say to you. Who wants to think that much? I just want to live my life and be happy. You can live your life just as you are doing now, but if you react (do the first thing you think of in a situation) instead of respond (think clearly how you will handle a situation) to everything and if you play the role of victim versus heroine you never will be happy. But once you look inside your mind —once you begin to expand your mind—it opens up unlimited opportunities. Remember, as a victim you will always feel trapped; as a heroine (or hero) you will always have courage.

And to continue with the quote "Cause I believe you could change your mind and change our lives". I first thought the words were "I believe you could change your mind and change your life" but I checked a couple sources and it is not "your life" but "our lives." Perhaps the writers did this because we are all connected. And while I constantly preach to others and believe we only have control over our life, we can't change others; the truth is our life does affect others. A Mother or Father who plays the victim role will probably pass that trait on to their children. We learn by observing, and if we can change our mindset to eliminate the victim mentality, there are probably people in our life who will benefit from us doing this. We CAN change our lives by using our minds to control our thoughts— which determine our feelings and lead us to our actions.

CHALLENGE

I encourage you to listen to the song
"Your Life is Now" by John Mellencamp.
But the challenge is to uncover if there is
an area of your life where you play the victim
and start to change your mindset.
Become aware of when and where you are doing this and
try to switch your role from victim to Hero or Heroine.

Use the following space to write down your thoughts on this chapter.

___

___

___

___

chapter six

COMPARISON

"Comparison is the thief of joy."

– Theodore Roosevelt

Social media has made comparing ourselves to others easier than ever. We are constantly exposed to pictures of people having what looks to be so much fun. It's a snapshot of a single second in time, but if we do not realize this, we can start to compare our life to theirs and feel inadequate. I overheard someone call Facebook, Fakebook once and although I chuckled at the remark, I can see how that name could be used by people who know the truth behind some of the pictures and posts. Facebook is a wonderful platform because it allows us to stay in touch but it can allow for "fake" comparisons and steal our joy if we allow it.

When we compare ourselves to others, we often feel bad about ourselves and we rarely feel joy. We either start thinking we're not good enough, or we feel resentment of some kind. I am the first one to admit, I used to compare myself to others all the time. I'm not even sure I knew I was doing it, but I do know I had a sadness in me that I couldn't quite figure out why. I now know it was in part because of the comparisons in my mind I was making between my life and others. I remember when someone would tell me some good news, something great that just happened to them. Of course, I was happy at the moment, but when I was alone I would think about it and ask "how come that didn't happen to me?", "Why do they have all the luck?" I used to be envious of people who had a nicer car than I had, or what I thought was a better job. I was jealous of people who had more money than me, or who had what I thought was the ideal life. What I've learned though is when we compare, we are often led to despair and this never is a good thing.

But about ten years ago I discovered a key that changed my way of looking at my own life and looking at what others had compared to what I had. The key that unlocked a world of new possibilities was the realization that the world is full of unlimited possibilities and abundance. It is. And that is the best news ever. Just because someone has something, it doesn't take it away from you. You can have it too. There's no scarcity, it's all in our minds. Someone else's good future is not your misfortune. You can have anything you want. You just have to know what it is, make a plan and go after it.

We often want what someone else has but we don't want to do the work to get it. If we're not willing to do the work why are we jealous of them because they did?

Notice the next time you start feeling jealous or envious of someone else. What were you thinking right before you felt this way? Were you comparing yourself to them? There's no need to do this. Start believing you can have anything you want, because you can if you are willing to do the work.

Are you going to let comparison steal your joy? Or are you going to remember the world is full of unlimited abundance and get out there and claim yours? Remember: You hold the power to your happiness.

CHALLENGE

Start thinking and believing in unlimited abundance!
When you recognize you are starting to
compare yourself to someone else, stop.

If you literally have to say the words
out loud "stop" then do it.

Use the following space to write your thoughts down on any comparisons you have made recently that have stolen your joy.

Do you believe in unlimited possibilities and abundance? Why or why not?

chapter seven

FEELINGS

> *"No one can make you feel inferior without your consent."*
>
> – Eleanor Roosevelt

This quote is so true yet I hear people all the time making comments like "they make me feel stupid"or " they make me feel guilty" or "they make me feel awful"; the adjectives we use to describe how others supposedly make us feel are endless. But here's the thing, just like Mrs. Roosevelt says— it's YOU that are giving THEM permission to make you feel this way. Our feelings come from our thoughts. If you think they're making you feel a certain way, they're NOT, it's your thought that is making you feel this way.

Our thoughts are not all true either. When you blame someone else for how you feel, your thought is coming from your interpretation of what they said. It could be the most trivial comment, like for example someone could say to you "can you please remember to lock the door when you leave the house"and that comment could be interpreted by you as "they think I'm irresponsible"or "they think I'm stupid, why would I need to be reminded to do that". Or instead of taking their comment defensively, you could think, "that's just them, they're paranoid about the house being locked" and not give their comment another thought or feeling. Often what people say is more about them and less about you.

I know, it's so much easier to blame someone else for how we feel, isn't it? "They don't appreciate me" you may remark after doing something special for someone when you don't get the reaction you thought you would from them. Or you may tell a friend " they make me feel bad about myself" as you are telling them a story about how your boss suggested a different way for you to get your work done. Do you find yourself ever saying anything like this? I have. But then I have to remind myself it's just my thought that is causing me angst. Whatever they did or said to me is fact, but how I interpret it is fiction. Two people can hear the same words and take them totally differently. What I may take offense to, someone else may not and visa versa. Here's another mind exercise: picture the person who said what made you think "they make me feel bad about myself" apologizing and telling you they're so sorry they treated you terribly. Imagine whatever suck up apology you want from them and then consider how you would feel. Would you feel better? If you would, your "better" feeling is coming from a "better" thought. If you think they are being sincere your thought and feeling will be different then if you don't. Do you now understand how your thoughts create your feelings?

Having said this though, we are more apt to get upset when we think what someone says has some truth in it. For example, if someone told me "I hate your pink hair", I'd think they were crazy because I don't have pink hair. Their comment wouldn't bother me at all. But, if I think their comment has some truth in it, for example, if they proclaimed "you always have to have things neat and tidy" I may take offense, because I am a bit of a neat freak. But knowing now this secret, that our thoughts create our feelings, I would no longer be offended or upset over this comment because I would realize they are right and to be upset over it would be giving them the power to upset me. As kids we learned "sticks and stones can break my bones but names can never hurt me". It's true. It's all how we interpret the words that are said to us. The words themselves can't hurt unless you allow them.

Do you understand Eleanor Roosevelt's quote "No one can make you feel inferior without your consent" better now? I hope so. Don't give people the power to make you feel a certain way. You get to decide what your thought is going to be and how you feel. If you want to be upset, you can be upset, just own it. Don't blame them for making you feel a certain way. Your new thought could be "how I'm deciding to think about what they said to me makes me feel upset and I'm ok with my decisions to feel this way".

CHALLENGE

Become more aware of when, or if you are allowing,
what someone else says or does
to make you feel a certain way.
Awareness is important.
And then if you want to try to feel better about it,
choose a different thought.

Are there people in your life who make you feel a certain way? Do you understand now how it is just your thought about what they said that makes you feel this way?

Use the following space to write down anything you want on this chapter.

chapter eight

THE EGO

> *"The ego takes everything personally."*
>
> \- Eckert Tolle

Our ego, our sense of self esteem, plays a big part of how we think and ultimately feel. Let's start this chapter with a few questions to get your mind stretched and please try to answer them honestly. I say this because the ego also likes to lie, it doesn't want to ever admit it has flaws so honesty only comes from our soul, not our ego.

Do you hate being told you are doing something wrong? If someone suggests a different way of doing something do you get angry, flustered or annoyed they are even bringing it up? And speaking of annoyed, how often do you get annoyed at others? Do you take things much too personally and then blame how you feel on another person? If you answered yes to any of these, this is your ego reacting, and not your soul responding to others. Our egos cannot stand it when we are wrong, our ego does not want to even think about being wrong and therefore what often happens is our ego will react quickly. It may blurt out something in anger, it may stew about something someone said that hurt our feelings (which you now know comes from your thought about what they said) and our ego is actually fearful that others don't see us in a perfect light. Our ego loves to argue with others and to challenge others.

But when we can become aware of our ego and start to recognize when our ego is talking to us (also known as giving us thoughts); we can then realize it's not giving us the best advice. We can then learn to put our ego aside in making our decisions, and start responding instead of reacting to situations. And, once we start to do this, we will begin to have more peace in our lives.

Back in 1985 over 40 of the biggest recording stars of the time came together to record a song to benefit Africa. The song was "We Are the World" and it was written by Michael Jackson and Lionel Ritchie and it was produced by Quincy Jones. I read back then that Quincy Jones made a sign and hung it on the door of the recording studio which read "Please Check Your Ego at the Door". I love that over 30 years ago Quincy Jones knew the power and the detriment the ego can have on people. Gathered at the studio were the biggest recording stars at the time being told your ego is not welcome here; we need each of you to come together and work together. That's why our ego is not our friend. Our ego doesn't want to work with others, it wants to alienate us from others. It wants to say: "I know more than you"; "I have to have things my way"; "I'm only happy when I get my way". The ego doesn't care about peace or harmony, the ego only cares about itself.

On a side note— you can feed someone's ego by telling them how wonderful they are. It's true, you can. My Mom actually told me on my wedding day the key to a happy marriage is you need to feed your husband's ego everyday. I'm not going to divulge what else she said was the key to happy marriage but my parents were married for over 70 years and she has way more wisdom than I ever gave her credit for growing up. If you want to feed someone's ego go ahead. We all like our ego fed now and then. You now know though you are just saying kind words and it's all their own thought about what you said that makes them feel good.

CHALLENGE

Notice when your ego is talking to you.
Start to be aware of when your thoughts
are coming from your ego.
And, if you want , escort your ego out the door.

Use the following space to write down your thoughts on this chapter.

____
____
____
____
____
____
____
____
____
____
____
____
____
____

chapter nine

DECISIONS

> *"The more you love your decisions,*
> *the less you need others to love them."*
>
> – Author Unknown

Decisions. We make them every day. Some decisions are big and some are small. Some we agonize over for days, weeks and even months. Some we make in a split second. Our big decisions are often the decisions we don't want to make alone. For these big decisions, we want insight from someone we respect and care about. We want to hear what they think we should do. It's perfectly normal to want to do this. But if you really stop and think about the decisions you make, do you need others to love your decisions more than you do?

This quote reminds me of all the times in my past when I had to make a decision, big or small. I would literally take a poll among anyone I could get to listen to me, and find out their opinion on it before I would make my decision. I'm sure I drove some people crazy doing this. In hindsight I think I did this so I could get the majority of people to agree with what I really wanted in the first place. I needed them to provide validation for the decision I actually wanted to make. If the first few people didn't give me the answer I really wanted, I just kept asking until enough people told me what I wanted to hear. Is anyone else guilty of this? Deep down we know what decision we want to make, but we also want everyone to agree with us. So we drive people crazy with our polling. We don't realize the power we have within us. Don't give away your power to others by worrying about what they will think of your decision. You know yourself better than anyone. You know what is best for you and you hold the power to decide what is best for you.

How do we start to love our decisions? I think we first need to begin by feeling more confident in ourselves. How can we do this? By stop fearing we will make the wrong decision. No decision is wrong and there are very few decisions that are 100% permanent. I'm not advocating that you should go into every decision thinking you're going to change it, but it is a bit calming to realize you can if you want to. Instead of polling people or worrying about what others think of your decisions, use your own power to start making decisions on your own. Start to be decisive instead of indecisive. Indecisiveness wastes so much time. Time we can never get back, and it leads to what is called "the paralysis of analysis". We start to dwell on all the different outcomes of our decision and that can drive us nuts and waste more time.

CHALLENGE

The next time you have a decision to make and you normally would ask a few people their opinion about it, try to make the decision yourself.

It may seem scary so have patience with yourself,
but try it at least once this week
and see how you feel once you do.
Start to LOVE your decisions.

Use the following space to write down some decisions you have to make and your thoughts on these decisions. You will learn a lot by writing down your thoughts.

chapter ten

INDECISION

> *"Indecision is the enemy of progress."*
>
> - Author Unknown

This quote resonated with me when I saw it as I find many people these days stuck in indecision. And, it made me start to think why is this? Why do many of us have a hard time making a decision? Well the answer may seem obvious—it could be we're afraid of making the wrong decision so we conclude no decision is better than the wrong decision. Or is it? Which do you think is worse—staying in indecision or making a wrong decision?

I used to be very indecisive. I hated making any kind of decision at all. I grew up the youngest of six so a lot of decisions in our house, even trivial things like what we were going to watch on TV, were made by my older siblings or parents. Nobody really asked me my opinion on things, so I never had to make decisions until I went to college. And then, when I could, when I was free to do so, I couldn't. I was so scared to make a decision on my own. So I would often wait and make no decision at all. Here's an example, I hated by first job out of college. I was bored to tears and I knew it was not what I wanted to be doing with my life, but the thought of leaving and figuring out what I wanted to do was too scary to think about. I knew I wanted to leave but I also couldn't think about how I was going to—what would be my next step—my next career. So I stayed for eight long years—I couldn't make that decision to leave when I knew one year into the job that it wasn't for me. And, the only reason I eventually left was to move to New York City to be closer to my boyfriend at the time. If he hadn't come along, who knows if I'd still be in that job. I'd like to think I wouldn't be but leaving it changed me, it made me grow and although things with him didn't work out, it made me who I am today and for that I am grateful.

So here's the thing about indecision, it really doesn't have any good qualities to speak of. Think about it, have you ever heard anyone ever comment "I'm indecisive and loving every minute of it"? Or, "I'm so glad I'm being indecisive right now"? No of course you haven't. Because being indecisive is like trying to balance on water with your left foot in one canoe and your right in another. You're not committing to getting into one boat or the other and you're about to fall over. Indecision is just like this. You're trying to make a decision while straddling two different options. You're exhausted and you are also making no progress!

As long as we're indecisive, we are going nowhere. We're at a stalemate. But why do we choose to be in this state of limbo? I think it comes back to fear of making the wrong decision, which I get into more later in this book under the Chapter Failure is an Option. Remember indecision can paralyze us and make us think if we make the wrong decision the world is going to end. We think we will never be able to recover from our decision, and there's a million other things our brain tells us because it doesn't want us to exert too much energy, it doesn't want us to think too hard. So it doesn't care when we're in a state of indecision. It tells us to take our time, we don't need to make a decision right now. This delay can cause us to eventually wake up and realize we've gone nowhere because we can't make a decision. We waste so much time and energy being indecisive.

Full disclosure here, I by no means am the master of making decisions. I too am indecisive at times. But I'm learning to catch myself sooner and try to steer myself into making a decision. Even small indecisions I find are a waste of time. The place I notice I'm currently most indecisive in is the grocery store. There's too many flavors these days, what the heck is going on? The potato chip aisle was confusing enough for me when all I had to decide was between no salt, low salt or rippled; but now we have a whole slew of flavors, including lobster roll by Lay's (they are delicious by the way). I can stand in that aisle for five minutes staring at all the options and trying to decide which I want to try. A waste of time for sure and something I am working on.

CHALLENGE

Start to realize when you're being indecisive
and try to make a decision.
Begin with an easy decision,
like my example in the grocery store.
Try to then be more decisive
with another decision, and build on that.
Remember "Indecision is the Enemy of Progress".

Use the following space to write down any thoughts you have on this chapter.

___

___

___

___

chapter eleven

H.A.L.T.

HUNGRY
ANGRY
LONELY
TIRED

HALT is an acronym and you should not make any decision when you are under the influence of any one or more of these feelings.

Start stretching your mind and think about this acronym. Do you agree with it? Did one of them stand out more than another? Recently I was in a bad mood and talking with my husband about it. I told him I was in a funk and I couldn't put my finger on why. He didn't skip a beat and commented "you're hungry and tired" I can tell. And you know what, he was right. I had stayed up late the night before; it was past lunchtime and I hadn't eaten yet and when I am tired or hungry I let little things annoy me, so I was angry too. I was actually three of these four adjectives! Luckily the only decision I had to make right then was where to go grab a bite to eat.

What about you? What are you like, what do you do when one of these strike? Do you get moody or do you snap at others when you are hungry or tired? Do you shut down when you are angry? Can you think of any decisions you've made when you've been experiencing one of these? How did it go? Let's start with the first adjective hungry. When we're hungry, even our decision on what to eat is different from when we are not. Making a decision on what to buy at the grocery store when I'm hungry, even though I have a list, is totally different for me from when I go there when I'm not.

Expand your mind some more and try to remember the last time you were angry. Maybe it was yesterday or maybe it was five minutes ago. What did you do? I find when I'm angry it's best to keep my mouth shut around others. I don't say anything good or productive when I'm angry. I'm not ok with being angry. There are people though who remark "I'm angry but I'm ok". If they are angry and they're going to forget about their anger and move on, that's great. But I feel people comment "I'm angry but I'm ok" just to show they're tough or because they don't want others to worry about them. But, the truth is they aren't ok and they won't be ok if they're going to remain angry. That's when they may need to HALT. They're angry, so they should avoid making any decision while they are in this state of mind. And so should all of us.

What's your mindset when you're lonely? Do you feel up to making a decision when you're feeling this way? Think about what makes you feel lonely. Is it just when you're alone you feel lonely? I can feel lonely even when I'm in a crowd. I worked in NYC for a brief period and I still remember feeling so alone as I walked the streets home at night. I was in a city with literally millions of people, and yet I felt totally alone. When we're feeling lonely we are usually vulnerable and making a decision when we are vulnerable is never a good thing. So another time we need to HALT is when we're lonely.

And now on to the last adjective, tired. Have you ever made a decision out of sheer exhaustion, maybe even exhaustion from thinking about what you had to make a decision about? I'm sure there are some parents out there who have at one time or another just given in to their child's request because they're too tired to argue anymore. When we're tired we're not thinking clearly so it's automatically not a good time to make any decision. Add any of these other adjectives-hungry, angry or lonely and you've got yourself a double, triple or quadruple dose of bad decision making ingredients. HALT and wait until you are feeling better before you make a decision, you will be glad you did.

CHALLENGE

HALT! Begin to recognize when you are
Hungry, Angry, Lonely or Tired
and don't make any decisions when you are one
or a combination of any of these adjectives.

If you're hungry, go get something to eat.
If you're angry, work on calming yourself down.
If you're lonely, call a friend or watch a funny movie.
If you're tired, get some rest.

Do something to help yourself,
but HALT from any decisions.

Use the following space to write your thoughts on this chapter.

___

___

___

chapter twelve

HABITS

> *"Our habits decide our future."*
>
> – Author unknown

We all have habits. Some we are glad we have, others we may want to break. Begin stretching your mind and think about your own personal habits. You probably have dozens of them, some you're not even aware of. But if I were to ask you which ones have the capability to help your future self what would you say? Do you make it a habit to go to the gym and work out? That's definitely helping your future self if you do. Do you make it a habit to save a little money every paycheck? That's a habit that helps determine our future. If we don't save, what will we live on once we retire? What about if you keep your house or your car clean and kept up. If you keep them in the best shape you will hopefully get a better return on your investment when you sell them in the future than if you did not keep them in good shape. So your "habit" of cleaning your house, or vacuuming your car is helping decide your future return on them. Even our habit of brushing our teeth several times a day will hopefully keep us from having to have a lot of dental work done and decide the future health of our teeth.

But now I want you think about any bad habits you may have. We all have them. Is there a bad habit you've been trying to kick and just can't seem to? One of mine is sweets, I have a terrible sweet tooth. I know it's not good for me, I know that too much sugar is not helping my future self. There's even some studies which suggest it causes Alzheimer's disease, and my Dad passed away from this disease last summer. But, even though I know it's bad for me; I just can't seem to resist a soft ice cream cone in the summer, or a dessert when we are out to dinner. I know this bad habit could determine a future that I don't want and therefore I need to cut down on my sugar intake. I've now taken that bad habit and turned it around into a positive one. I've made it a habit to look at the sugar content on most things I buy at the grocery store. It takes a little more time, but it's amazing to me how much sugar is in things I never thought of, like soup and sauce and even granola. I thought I was eating a healthy breakfast of greek yogurt, blueberries and granola till I saw the grams of sugar in the granola I was using. I now look at the labels on most products I use and I'm often shocked at the amount of sugar that is in some brands and even in different flavors by the same brand. And by doing this, I now buy the brand or the flavor with the least amount of sugar. A small habit like this can make a big difference. By reducing this sugar intake, by making it a "habit" to check labels, I'm helping my future self be more healthy.

What are some other bad habits people have which don't help their future selves? Smoking I think we all could agree is one. Smoking does not help anyone's future self and in fact often decides a bleak future for those who continue to do so. But, it's a hard habit to break for those who do smoke. Drinking heavily is another bad habit, as is any addiction.

The good news is any bad habit can be broken. We have the power to break any bad habit we have. We are the one in control, do not blame a bad habit on anyone else. Keep your power, do not give it away by saying it is out of your control. Good habits, bad habits—what kind of future do you want?

CHALLENGE

Look at your daily habits and determine which are helping and which are hurting your future. For any that are not helping your future self, decide what you need to do to kick these habits and begin doing so.

Are there any good habits you want to incorporate into your life? Use the following space to write down any good habits you have or want to have, and also any bad habits you want to break.

Good habits:

___

___

___

___

___

___

___

___

___

___

___

Bad habits:

chapter thirteen

COMMUNICATION

> *"The single biggest problem with communication is the illusion it has taken place."*
>
> – George Bernard Shaw

You know what I find interesting? We have more modes of communication now than ever before and yet it seems like we are having fewer and fewer conversations. We currently can communicate using email, text message, Facebook, Instagram, Twitter and Snap Chat, just to name a few. We think we're doing a good job communicating, and we are; sort of. But, we've allowed these other forms of communication to replace basic human interactions. Texting and Email has made our life easier on so many levels but it still can be misconstrued and can be interpreted many different ways depending on who is reading it. We may be "connecting" more with people on a technological level, but we are "disconnected" on a personal level. With these new quick and instant forms of communication, the writing is abbreviated and important details are either omitted or they are often misread by those on the receiving end.

With so many different forms of communication, we often forget which one we used to send out the information. Have you ever found yourself talking with someone trying to figure out whether the information you sent them was on a text or an email? Do you at times think you communicated something to someone and they said you never told them? Do you think because you post something on social media every person you want to know about it, see's it? They don't. Facebook & Instagram all have algorithms and unless someone is paying to boost a post, you only see about 10% of what is posted from your group of "friends".

What I am seeing with the increase use of these communication platforms is fewer people picking up the phone or engaging in face to face conversations. We may get annoyed when someone doesn't know about something that we think is important or we may get upset if they interpret the email or text we sent in a way we didn't intend. But when this happens do you try to pick up the phone to talk to them about the misinterpretation or do you try to clarify the problem using the same form of communication that caused the misinterpretation? Would the miscommunication have been avoided if you picked up the phone and called them or had a conversation with them face to face?

And, while we are on the topic of communication, when we do get together with friends, family and even in a business setting, how many people have their cell phone close by, and they check them during the conversation or meeting? So here's a mind stretching exercise, if you are old enough, think back to before cell phones. Remember back then? Can you even image if you were talking with someone or if you were in a meeting and all of a sudden a person took out a sheet of paper and started to write a note to someone else who wasn't there in the middle of your conversation or meeting. Wouldn't you be appalled? Wouldn't that be considered rude? But it has become totally acceptable to be talking with someone and get a text and look at it. We don't even flinch now when someone does this. Some, if not most of us, do it too. We start to half listen to the conversation we are in, to respond to someone who isn't even with us, and we think it's rude not to respond right away. What I find interesting is we don't consider it rude to ignore the people we are with to tend to someone who is not with us.

Now that we've thought out this a bit, let's start to think about how we communicate and if we are doing so in the best possible way for no misinterpretation to take place. The next time you find yourself saying "that's not what I meant", think about how you could have avoided even saying that. Would it have been easier to call the person on the phone? Did they misinterpret or did you lack in explaining yourself? Remember: The biggest problem with communication is the illusion it has taken place" and I like to add "it's often misinterpreted if it's in an email or text."

CHALLENGE

Pick up the phone or talk to someone in person instead of sending them a text or an email. Before you start to type an email or text, if the person is in close proximity to you, get up and talk to them face to face.

Use the following space to write down your thoughts on this chapter.

____

____

____

____

chapter fourteen

JUDGEMENTS

> *"Do not judge anyone's story by the chapter you walked in on."*
>
> – Author Unknown

Let's talk about judgements, we all make them everyday. We live in a society that encourages them. From politicians to religious leaders, it seems everyone is pointing a finger at someone and proclaiming what they are doing is wrong and the finger pointer is right.

We learn at a young age about judging. Many of us were taught as children not to do this and to treat everyone fairly and with kindness but somehow as adults we forget this lesson and judge people without a second thought. Someone cuts us off in traffic, "What a jerk," we instantly think. We have no clue if they saw us or if they are in an emergency situation to get somewhere. We judge people by the clothes they wear, the cars they drive, the neighborhood they live in. We judge them by their attractiveness or not. Admit it, you have done this before at least once. We see a man or woman who is good looking and we often associate them with being nice, or on the flip side we may think that because they are good looking they must be stuck up. The point is before we even get to know someone, we automatically start judging them.

We don't like it when we're being judged, but we don't see it as quite as bad when we are doing the judging. We think we're just making an observation. But have you ever made an observation before you knew all the facts? Have you ever said

"I don't think they should do that"? (I'm not sure what "they" were going to "do" but I know when I have said this, I was judging the person.) Whether consciously or subconsciously, I was putting my two cents into the mix and very often I did not have the full story.

Well, it's human nature right? Or is it? And even if it is, do you want to stop? If you don't I'm not judging you. You can be whoever you want to be. Judge away. But if you want to try stop judging others or if you even want to wean yourself off this habit, really think about this quote and how it may relate to a recent judgement you made on someone else. What chapter did you walk in on in this person's life? Sometimes we make a judgement and then someone tells us something about the person's past and we immediately change our judgement and say "I didn't know that." Because we now know more of their story, we are suddenly less judgmental. Why did we have to be told whatever it was before we suddenly change our thought about them? Why can't we try to think in a more positive way about people? If someone is rude, instead of judging them harshly why can't we just think, "They must be having a hard day, I hope whatever is bothering them works out." I've had people tell me about bad service they had at a restaurant. They may have loved the food and the atmosphere, but they didn't think the wait staff was attentive enough and they write the place off forever. One time, zero tolerance is what we sometimes give people instead of a second chance. We all have bad days, bad moments, things we've done and said that we wish we could take back.

We gain nothing when we judge others. There's no upside to doing it, for them or us. We all have flaws, we all are human and we all make mistakes. Let's try to replace our judgements with compassion.

CHALLENGE

The next time you are about to
make a judgement about someone,
stop it if it's going to be a negative one.
You don't need to say what you were going to say.
Try not to think about your judgement either.
You may not have the full story and all the facts.
Remember: don't judge people
by the chapter you walked in on.

Have you judged anyone recently? Use the following space to write down your thoughts on this chapter.

chapter fifteen

AGREEING TO DISAGREE

> *"We need to learn to get along with others even though we disagree with others."*
>
> \- Annette Q

This quote came to me as I was having a conversation with a friend who is an office manager. She was concerned about two employees who do not get along because they have different opinions on how some tasks should be done. It had gotten so bad that one employee refused to share an item his co-worker needed to complete her work. My friend's story made me respond "they need to learn to get along with each other even though they disagree with each other".

I bet everyone would agree with this statement; it sounds simple enough. But somehow, somewhere between kindergarten and adulthood, we at times forget this golden rule and start believing we don't need to get along with others. We start believing our viewpoint is the correct viewpoint and people who do not agree with us are wrong. We get set in our ways. We become agitated with people who don't share the same opinion as us. And, we are often frustrated unnecessarily because of this.

If you don't want to be around people who don't agree with you on things, that's your choice, but you're going to lead a very lonely life if you start alienating people whose views are different from yours. It's impossible to agree on everything with everyone all the time. So how do we get a long with others when our opinions are different? I believe the answer to this question is tolerance. Remember tolerance? Our desire for instant gratification provided by the technology we have at our fingertips may be responsible for losing our ability to tolerate others. Tolerance requires time and thought. The definition of tolerance according to the American Heritage Dictionary is: "The capacity for or the practice of recognizing and respecting the beliefs or practices of others. "

Start stretching your mind and think about the people in your life you just can't stand to be around. Maybe some are family members, hopefully distant family members, or co-workers you don't see eye to eye with, or a neighbor or casual "friend". Maybe you don't see them often but you still can't get along with them. Is it because their views on a few matters are different from yours, and so what if they are? Aren't they allowed their own opinion and how does their opinion affect you? Now I understand some people can be annoying but what if we try to be tolerant of them and maybe remark "I know we have a difference of opinion on this so can we agree to disagree and move forward?" or some version of those words.

It's ok to disagree with someone and it's perfectly acceptable to have a voice and tell them. What's damaging is when we don't work on getting along with them when we need to, like the bickering co-worker at the beginning of the chapter. Do you find yourself being short or having little patience with certain people and if so, is it because you may have had a disagreement with them in the past? Do you justify your lack of tolerance towards them by telling yourself and maybe others that they're just plain crazy or mean or stupid? Try recognizing your way is not the only way and it's ok someone has a different opinion than yours. You will start to notice your tolerance towards others has increased along with your ability to accept their differences.

CHALLENGE

Practice tolerance towards others
whose opinions are different from yours.
Instead of being frustrated they don't see things
exactly as you do, try to have tolerance for their viewpoint,
even try to understand it from their perspective.
And if you still don't understand it,
just agree to disagree.

Use the space below to list people who have different views than you. What area of your life does this difference affect you?

____

____

____

____

____

____

____

____

____

____

____

chapter sixteen

AWAKEN TO YOUR OWN WORLD

> *"We're mentally running the world, and we're asleep to our own."*
>
> – Byron Katie

Byron Katie is an American speaker and author who teaches a method of self-inquiry known as"The Work by Byron Katie" or simply as "The Work". I first heard this quote during her interview with Oprah in which she was discussing situations that are your business versus situations that are none of your business. We will further discuss the none of your business concept in the next chapter. For this chapter we are going to delve a little deeper and explore Katie's intriguing quote.

Let's start by stretching our mind and thinking about all the things we consciously think about throughout the day. This morning when you got up, what was your first thought? Was it about something you had to do or about what you needed someone else to do? Was it about making the kids lunches or that you forgot the dry cleaning or an upcoming meeting at work, or how you needed to cancel an upcoming lunch with a friend and you forgot? Like me do you listen to the News and comment on what is being reported? All of this is exactly what Byron Katie is saying: we are mentally running the world and asleep to our own world. Instead of concentrating on our lives, we are spending mental energy on others. Our thoughts are about other people's business and not our own. Byron Katie is trying to get us to be in our own business!

Here's a visual exercise for you—if you take the hours you are awake and all your thoughts and put them in a circle, what percent of that circle is thoughts you are having that have to do with you? If you visualize that circle as a pie, how big of a piece of pie are you spending on thoughts of yourself—your world—how to make your life better versus time you spend thinking about others? Now that you can see this, are you ready to let go of thoughts about other people's business? Are you ready to be awakened to you?

Some people don't want to do this. It's easier to concentrate on others. There's no accountability when our thoughts are about others. We can judge them or we can sympathize with them. We can think whatever we want and we don't have to do anything but just do that. But when our thoughts are about us, about our world, we then become accountable to ourselves and that is often a hard thing to do. Looking at ourselves, our own life, is a lot more work. We may realize we need to change if we want to move forward in our life, and change is scary. We're creatures of habit, change is the opposite of habit.

How do you begin to spend your mental energy on yourself and how do we shift our mental energy when we realize we're wasting it? Here is an example which may help. Let's pretend you are in a meeting and you think the meeting is a waste of your time. Your mind starts racing and asking "who put this meeting together, why do I have to be here" etc. As you are thinking these thoughts you feel yourself getting antsy. Your impatience starts rising up inside of you, your heart rate may start to increase and all you want is to be out of there—fast.

After all, you're thinking, you're a busy person and have a lot to do. What I want you to understand is you are mentally running the world right now. You are figuring out everything that is wrong with this meeting. You can't change the fact you are there, but your mind is consumed by the fact you are there and you don't need to be. You can shift this energy and instead use your mind to figure out what you need to know or learn in this meeting. You can stop mentally criticizing and start paying attention. Or if you really don't believe you need to be in the meeting, you can use the time to think about what needs to be done when you get out of the meeting. No one has to know you are doing this, just use the time to your advantage. We can shift a thought to our advantage once we are aware of our thoughts. If we are asleep to our thoughts we can't.

CHALLENGE

Take notice of when you are
"mentally running the world
and you are asleep to your own".
Shift your energy from what you can't control
to what you can. Start running your own world.

Use the following space to write down your thoughts on this chapter.

---

chapter seventeen

NONE OF YOUR BUSINESS

> *"If it's none of your business,*
> *don't make it your business."*
>
> – Annette Q

I can't begin to tell you how much more peace I experience in my day when I adhere to this message. I have to admit, it is not easy at times. Without even realizing it, we get involved in "business" that is not ours. So to recognize when we are doing this, I'm going to ask you to answer the following questions. How many times during the day do you interject your opinion when no one asked your opinion? Do you ever find yourself giving advice to someone who never asked for it? Have you ever overheard a conversation and offered your advice because you were sure you knew what they were talking about, but you were wrong? You thought you were being helpful but they were annoyed you broke into their conversation. And one more question for you as we begin this chapter: How often do you find yourself uttering the words "I was just trying to be helpful" or a version of those words?

As humans, we like to be helpful. Therefore, we naturally interject our thoughts into conversations when we think we can help. While we justify our actions by telling ourselves we're being a good person, being nice, looking out for our fellow man; if no one asked us in the first place, we may want to look into why we feel the need to get involved in what may be none of our business. You can disagree with me—you can say it is your business because it involves your spouse, or your kids or whoever it's about. And you can continue to do so if that's what you want to do. We are adults and we can do whatever we want.

All I can relay to you is what I have learned from my personal experience. When I look back at situations where I gave my advice or interjected what I knew because I wanted to be helpful, but I was never asked, I don't think my input was appreciated too much. I have found more peace staying silent in situations where before, without being asked, I gave my two cents. Why? Because if you continue to stretch your mind and think about it, how many times when you gave advice without being asked did the person you gave it to agree you were right? What percentage of the time did they thank you or appreciate your help? Most of the time if our opinion wasn't asked the person we're giving advice to probably isn't going to take our advice anyway and we get frustrated while they get annoyed.

I'll give you a couple examples to help distinguish when something is our business or when it's not our business. One morning this winter my husband needed to plow our driveway and our neighbors driveway because we had a pretty significant snowfall overnight. I was about to ask him if he had texted her to let her know when he would get to her driveway. My thought was he should give her some advance notice in case she needed to get out sooner than he planned on plowing her driveway. But, I caught myself and didn't ask the question. The reason was, it really wasn't my business. The agreement they have over his service in plowing her driveway has nothing to do with me. So, if I was to ask him and if his answer was "no" (which I was pretty certain it was going to be) I knew I would be frustrated over this. And I knew I would tell him I think he should give her a "heads up" on when he plans to plow her out. And, I'm sure he would have been annoyed at me for telling him what I think he needs to do. It really doesn't matter what I think. It's not my business. Even if I was just trying to be helpful to her—or to him—it's not my business. I avoided a potential disagreement between my husband and me by keeping my mouth shut.

Another example of what is none of my business is after a meeting I overheard some people discussing the quickest way to get somewhere. They were contemplating what roads they should take, what the traffic was going to be like, etc. I was not part of this initial discussion, I just happened to hear it as I was walking by and I did have my opinion on the best way to go. I had my opinion and even my personal experience on these roads but...I just kept on walking. Why? Because their discussion was None of My Business - they were not asking me what I thought as I walked by. I might think I know the best way, but it's just my thought. Maybe some of you think this is being anti-social or not helpful, but I can tell you trying to mind my own business has freed up some time and energy for me that I never knew I was missing.

Byron Katie whose quote I used last chapter explains in her book <u>Loving What Is</u> there's 3 types of business: There's My Business, which is something that involves me obviously; there's Our Business, which is something that involves me and you, or me and someone else; and then there's None of My Business; which is something I am not involved in and I should keep out of. I also like the expression "Stay in Your Own Lane". Think of this as an example next time you are getting involved in what may be none of your business. If you are driving down the road and your car goes into another lane, you may cause an accident. If we "stay in our own lane" we are usually guaranteed safe travels. This is providing we keep our head up and are aware of our surroundings. And of course, if no one else comes into our lane. The same with life, everyone needs to stay in their own lane. Stay in your own lane and you will probably keep moving forward safely. Cross over the line and go into the other lane and you may be headed for disaster.

CHALLENGE

Recognize or write down below when a situation
is your business or none of your business.
Try to stay in your own lane.
Start this practice for one day and see how many days
you can make it to before you go into another lane.
And, when you cross the line and get into the wrong lane,
just gently get back into your own.
It's ok you crossed the line, it's not a good idea
to continue driving in the wrong lane.
Keep your eyes on the road ahead of you and safe travels!

Use the space below to write down what is your business and what is none of your business.

My Business:

____

____

____

____

____

None of My Business:

chapter eighteen

EXCESS WEIGHT

> *"A lot of what weighs you down isn't yours to carry."*
>
> – Author Unknown

I may get some resistance on this and that's ok. Have an open mind and stop for a second and think about how often you worry about someone other than yourself. I used this example already but what percentage of your day is spent doing this? Did you come up with an actual percentage earlier?

Here's something else to think about: How many times throughout the day are you frustrated because you are thinking about what someone else should be doing, something they're not but you think they should? You may be thinking about a friend, a co-worker or a family member. Can you think of some examples? Any example, even one? And when you do, does it upset you if they are not doing what you think would be best for them? This is a perfect example of allowing something to weigh us down, that isn't ours to carry. We can't control others and yet we want to and we're often weighed down worrying about them. Our happiness is interrupted by frustrating thoughts of them. And, I'd be willing to bet if these same people knew you were worried about them they would tell you to stop worrying about them. They probably don't want you to, but you do anyway. You can't help yourself, you may say to yourself, or even them. But when we remark "I can't help myself" we're actually stating "I refuse to help myself". Replace the word "can't" with "won't" next time and do some mind stretching on that too. You can go back to Chapter 2 if you want to review this concept again.

Next question to ponder for this chapter is: Why do you worry more about others than about yourself? We all have people in our lives who we love dearly and of course we want what's best for them. But once they reach adulthood their life is theirs to lead and their decisions are theirs to own. It's difficult, hard, and even sad at times too when we think we know what's best for someone and they either don't want to listen or they do but ignore our advice. In these times especially we need to remind ourselves that just because we think we know what's best for someone doesn't mean it is. It's just our thought and we could be right or we could be wrong. We may not always agree with their decisions but worrying about them doesn't give them or you any peace. It's a hard concept to grasp but their burdens are not ours to carry—they're theirs. We can be there to support them emotionally —to listen to them if they need an ear to talk to— but we don't have to carry their burdens around with us and it doesn't help them or us to do so.

So what do you worry about and what weighs you down? Thoughts of our past, things that happened years ago that are over and done with can weigh us down too. And although they are real incidences that happened to us, it's your choice whether you want to continue to carry them and have them weigh you down.

Another good visual exercise is to make a list of what you're worried about right now. Maybe it's one thing, maybe it's multiple things. If you think of each item as a barbell which weighs 5 pounds, how many pounds are you carrying? And, once you figure how much weight you're carrying, figure out how many of those pounds are worries that are not really yours to carry. How many pounds of other people's problems are you bearing? Wouldn't you feel lighter if you got rid of some of this excess weight?

CHALLENGE

Use the space below to write down what you are currently worried about. Circle only those items that are yours to carry. Try for even one day to stop worrying about anything that is not circled.

chapter nineteen

LOSING MENTAL WEIGHT

> *"Sometimes the weight we need to lose isn't on our body."*
>
> – Author Unknown

As I mentioned in the forward of this book, the chapters have been arranged by topic and are not in the same sequence as my Podcast. Therefore, if this chapter sounds similar to the last, it is; but it's always helpful to review concepts more than once.

If you think grudges you hold, people you haven't forgiven from your past or even not forgiving yourself for mistakes you have made are not weighing you down, I ask that you really stretch your mind and be open to looking at them again. And, if you have an experience from your past that was not a good one, maybe it's from your childhood, maybe it's more recent like a relationship that went sour— and you retell that story over and over again, in your mind or to others—that is a huge weight that is probably weighing you down and you don't even realize it.

We all know people who never seem to be bothered by anything. They appear to be in a good mood all the time. They're fun to be around. The energy that surrounds them is positive and is almost contagious. You can't help but be in a good mood when you're around them. Could it be the reason why they are in a good mood is they don't let others, or experiences or their thoughts about these weigh them down? Maybe it is. Or maybe they are just in a good mood in front of others, but deep down they ARE bothered by some things. It's probably the latter, but it doesn't matter either way. It's unnatural to be happy 100% of the time. Brooke Castillo, a Life Coach I've had the pleasure of learning from says 50% of the time we are not going to be happy, and that's ok. What isn't ok, or what really keeps us down is not realizing our thoughts are causing our feelings whether we feel happy or sad. And whether you believe me or not, we DO have control over our thoughts and we could benefit from getting rid of thoughts that weigh us down.

The stories we tell ourselves in our minds as well as the stories we tell to others matter. They become who we are. It truly is amazing once you understand this and start to notice how your own thoughts control your feelings. You can then decide whether you want to continue a thought that is weighing you down. Try to notice next time you are telling a story and it's about something that makes you happy how your enthusiasm shines through. You may start to talk faster or your posture becomes more alert. In the same way, notice how your body responds when you are telling a story about something negative. You may whisper or talk a little softer, you may feel tired telling the story. Because your thoughts about it are not good, it is like a weight on your back.

So, what thoughts are weighing you down? What happened in your past that preoccupies your mind? Who in your life right now are you holding a grudge against? What has been bothering you this week? Did someone say something that hurt your feelings? Are you upset because you had an expectation involving someone else that wasn't met? And here's the most important question of all: How long are you going to hold on to your thoughts about this? I've left some space below to answer these questions and explore more about your thoughts. It really is your decision.

CHALLENGE

Find a weight you are willing to lose.
It may be a story from your past,
it may be anger you are holding
towards someone or even yourself.
And, next time your start to think about whatever it is,
say to yourself "no, I lost that weight, and it's staying off".

Thoughts that are Weighing you Down:

chapter twenty

A CLEAN SLATE

> *"Today is a clean slate,*
> *you can start over,*
> *right here, right now."*
>
> – Author Unknown

"Today is a Clean Slate, You Can Start Over, Right Here, Right Now" We've all heard this a hundred or thousands of times in different variations. Today is a New Day, Today is the First Day of the Rest of your Life. You know these cliches and most times we hear these words and carry on the way we always have. Do we ever stop and think: Yes that's right and I want to change something? I want to be a happier person today than I was yesterday. I want to start working towards that goal I have. With a clean slate we can choose to wipe away all the yesterdays we don't want; we can wipe away sadness from the past; we can choose to carry forward with us only thoughts that bring us joy. We can bring with us any memory we want. Special times with loved ones we don't ever want to forget, are examples of what we may choose to keep. We can choose however to not bring some memories with us. Embarrassing moments or other times we'd like to forget, we can discard.

Our mind is amazing, and it can store so much! We can recall things from all areas of our lives. We can remember our childhood days; we can remember our first kiss; we can remember where we were when an important event in history took place. But we also bring with us bad thoughts, bad feelings, bad memories from our past. These memories are on our old slate. And, we carry them around like old luggage. You've heard someone say, "Boy does Bill have a lot of baggage." We recognize it in others, but do we look within to see if we do this too? Often what we point out in others is a reflection back at us—we just don't realize it. Isn't this crazy? It is, but it's also being human, so don't beat yourself up over this.

What I want you to realize is you don't need to bring along the baggage of your past into a new day. You can start with a clean slate. You can fill the new slate with whatever you want. Here's a fun little exercise that takes no physical exertion. Think about all the luggage you have owned throughout your life. Think about the old heavy suitcases you used to have—some of you may remember even before luggage had wheels. And then luggage got wheels but it still wasn't as easy to maneuver as the high tech luggage we buy today.

For the second part of this exercise, visualize the various bad/sad/upsetting memories you have from various periods of your life and replace these with your old luggage. In your mind, just for a second, pick up your old luggage and visualize carrying it around with you. These pieces you've owned and now are old and not at all useful. Would you use them today if you were going on a trip? I doubt it. So why are you still carrying them around? You got rid of this old luggage because it no longer serves you. Why then are you keeping "mental baggage" that no longer is useful to you? Perhaps it's baggage you carry around everyday out of habit or maybe it's baggage you keep hidden until you feel like taking it out. We store our actual luggage in a closet, the basement or the attic of our home; we store "mental baggage" in the back of our minds. When we do take it out, we justify our actions by making up excuses like "you don't understand, when I was a kid this thing happened to me, that's why I'm hurt " or "I can't get over X".

If you are starting new with a clean slate (think of it as a new trip) do you really want to bring your old slate, your musty old luggage with you? You have a choice each day to start with a clean slate. Yesterday is gone, it's not coming back. You may wish it would, but it's not. Today is what you have. Think about what you truly want to bring with you to make it a beautiful day.

CHALLENGE

Think about getting rid of all your old baggage.

Try to start today and each day with a clean slate.

Put on that slate whatever brings you joy!

I promise if you do, you will feel so much better!

So much lighter!

Use the space below to jot down your thoughts on this chapter. What is on your clean slate for today?

chapter twenty-one

WORRYING

> *"99% of what you worry about never happens."*
>
> - Author Unknown

I'm not sure this quote is a scientific fact but I bet it is true! If what you're worrying about has a 99% chance of never coming to fruition why waste so much time and energy worrying about it? Some of us are programmed since childhood to worry. We observed it in others, when we were young, and so we naturally continue to do it as adults. It's what we know. It's what we're accustomed to. Instead of thinking everything is going to be ok, instead of looking on the bright side, we let our minds worry instead. Whether you worry a lot or a little, it is one of the biggest waste of time and energy and the most unproductive thing we can be doing. It is useless. It does not have one benefit to it.

Let's put worry into two categories and start stretching our minds. There's worrying about ourselves or worrying about others. We can start with self worry. Two questions to ask yourself are 1) What are you worried about? and 2) Why aren't you trying to change that worry into action? Are you worried about a job interview coming up, a relationship you may be in, a test result you are waiting for? Begin to identify what you are worried about. Then ask yourself instead of worrying is there something you could be doing instead? Is there an action you could be taking to help or change the situation? If there is you need to train your mind to take action, not sit and worry!

Write down in the spaces below 3 things that you are worried about and then name one action you can take for each instead of worrying.

I'm worried about:

___

___

___

___

___

___

___

___

___

Action to take instead:

___

___

___

___

___

___

___

___

___

Now let's talk about worrying about others. I believe my Mom has spent over half her life worrying, about one of her children and if you're a parent, chances are you have too. If you're not a parent, there's probably people in your life you worry about also. Here's the first question I have for you: Did anything you were worrying about ever actually happen? Maybe there's that 1% time it did and so you justify your worrying because of this small percentage. But when we're worried about others, we need to understand that we have no control over other adults and ultimately we are not responsible for their decisions, no matter how much we worry. So, instead of conjuring up terrible scenarios in your mind, why not spend time envisioning good things for them? For example you're worried about your husband driving home from a basketball game in a blizzard, You want him to be safe and you know there will be other crazed fans on the road. Instead of spending your time worrying about him buried in a ditch, why not spend that time envisioning him enjoying the game and smiling when he comes through the door? Why not train your mind to think of the positive outcome instead of the negative? Our brain can think about the positive just as much as the negative, we just need to train it to do so.

CHALLENGE

Recognize when you are worrying
and try to use that time more productively.
Create a mantra to think about instead.
A simple one is "All will be well"
but you can come up with your own.
Remember "99% of what you worry about never happens".
With those odds why do we spend
so much time on what will never happen?

Use the space below to write down your thoughts on this chapter.

chapter twenty-two

PROBLEMS

> *"Our problems are as big or as small as we choose them to be."*
>
> – Author Unknown

Do you agree with this quote? Or, do you believe there are some problems which are classified as big, and some which are classified as small? How do you determine what is a big problem or what is a small problem?

Get out your mental mat and think about a problem you have in your life right now. If I were to ask you "tell me what's bugging you today" how would you respond? Would you tell me about not getting the promotion you wanted at work or would you tell me about leaving your phone at home? What do you think is a problem in your life right now? By asking you "what do you THINK is a problem" I'm trying to help you recognize it's how we choose to look at things, whether they are big or small.

We all have problems or what I prefer to call obstacles in our life. Everything does not always go as planned and we all are faced with difficult situations at various times. But if we look at our problems and try to put them in perspective, we can often realize the truth in this quote. We do have a choice how we look at things. We can make a mountain out of a mole hill, as the old saying goes. I have a friend who uses the term "it's small potatoes, don't waste your time on it". She uses it when describing something that someone may perceive as a problem, but in the grand scheme of things, is actually not. She believes you shouldn't even put your energy into trying to figure out a solution to the problem. Maybe it's not our problem to begin with—it's someone else's problem but we start thinking about it like it is ours to figure out. If that's the case, we need to put an end to that quickly. Remember from chapter 17 "if it's none of your business, don't make it your business".

But what about a problem that does involve us? If we were to look at it in a different way could we possibly discover it's really not as big of a problem as we're making it out to be? Stuck in traffic and can't get to work on time? It could be a problem, maybe you have a meeting you should be at, maybe your boss is a tyrant and won't like the fact you're late. But, we can look at that as a small problem or a big problem. Some of you may classify it as a small problem, some would argue it's a big problem. But how YOU look at it is your choice. You can choose either way but if you choose to make it a small problem, a small obstacle, you will probably exert less energy on it. You may even just accept the fact you're stuck in traffic and there is nothing you can do about it. Acceptance of something out of our control can actually bring us peace. We may not like it, but accepting it as fact and moving on from thoughts on how to change it, can be freeing.

Here's something else to think about. Have you ever been talking with someone, it may even be someone you just met casually, and you were telling them about a problem you have and they disclose they had the exact same problem once? And, upon further discussion, you find out they didn't let whatever it is bother them at all, and, they can't really understand why you are? This is because we all see things differently, we all have different perspectives. What is a big deal to you may not be a big deal to someone else, and visa versa.

Stretch your mind way back to a problem you thought you had as a kid. Can you think back to what you saw as a big problem back then and now do you see it as not such a big deal? Maybe you dropped a nice glass in the kitchen and it broke, or you lost a library book. If you could tell your younger self something would it be not to look at it as such a big problem? Would you tell yourself not to fret, it will all work out?

We can also choose to look at a situation which most people would classify as a big problem and decide whether it's going to be a big problem in our life or not. Here's an example— Losing a job I think most of us would agree is a big problem. We start thinking about loss of income, bills we have to pay, taking care of our family, finding another job, the list goes on and on. But, some people I know have lost their job and they have had a much different perspective on it. They have actually told me "it's really the best thing to happen to me because it made me realize I wasn't doing what I want to do" or "it forced me to go out of my comfort zone and find a better job". I'm amazed when I hear this but I am also inspired when I do. It shows me the resilience people have. It also confirms the quote for this chapter.

Years ago I worked in an office building and my office was on the 5th floor. One Monday I was in the elevator going down to the main floor for something and I remember I was not in a good mood. Everyone in the elevator looked full of doom and gloom. The elevator was really quiet and then a man with crutches got on. He was smiling and his face was beaming as he said Hi to everyone on board. He seemed like he was in the best of moods, like he just won the lottery or something, despite the fact that the reason he was on crutches was he only had one leg! I can't recall why I was in a bad mood that day but

I do know when I saw this man being so happy, I thought to myself, "Wow you need to rethink your priorities and thank your lucky stars you have two legs to stand on." About a year later and in almost the identical scenario the same man got on the elevator but this time he was in a wheelchair because he lost his other leg in a motorcycle accident. Guess what though, he was still the most upbeat person on the elevator and continued to smile and talk to everyone. He really was an example of "Our problems are as big or as small as we choose them to be".

CHALLENGE

Decide what you are going to make
a big or small problem in your life this week.
Wouldn't it be great not to look at anything as a problem,
but instead look at any issue that arises
as an obstacle you just need to find a solution to?
And maybe, just maybe, the solution is to let it go.

Use the following space to write down your thoughts on this chapter.

What problems do you perceive as big?

What problems do you perceive as small?

chapter twenty-three

BEING COMFORTABLE WITH SILENCE

"Silence isn't empty. It's full of answers."

- Author Unknown

When was the last time you sat in complete silence—even just for five minutes? Have you ever even done this, sat without music or the TV on? Sat without reading a book or checking your phone? Sat completely by yourself, either inside or outside, maybe in a favorite room of your home or outside in the yard? Maybe in the background was the sound of nature—a bird singing or the wind blowing. But that was the only noise around—no sounds from other people or things.

If you've never done this, I highly recommend it and if you have but not recently, I urge you to do it again soon. In fact, why aren't we doing this more often? For those of you who are asking if what I'm talking about is similar to meditation, my answer is yes and no. The American Heritage Dictionary defines Meditation as "a devotional exercise of or leading to contemplation". I'm not declaring you need to meditate for hours, but I can tell you if you make sitting in silence for just five minutes a day a habit, you will become more calm and relaxed. Not a bad thing to try, huh?

Please don't respond you don't have the time, we're talking five minutes. If you say you don't have the time what you really mean is you don't want to. Which by the way is ok, but just be honest and not make excuses. And, If you don't want to spend five minutes in complete silence, can I suggest you dig a little deeper and answer the question why? What's the harm in doing it, even if it's just once? What is your reason, besides you just don't want to? You may uncover more when you answer that question.

When we sit in silence we can, just as the quote says, come up with answers that we may not when we are busy all the time. We may also gain more clarity on circumstances in our life.

For those of you who want to try sitting in silence I have some suggestions. Set your cell phone alarm for five minutes and then forget about it while you sit in silence. Don't keep looking at it to see how much time you have left. I did that the first time I tried this, which didn't give me the full benefit of the exercise at all. And remember to put the mute button on so you don't hear your texts or calls coming in. The alarm will still go off if you do this and the people that need to get in touch with you can wait five minutes. Before cell phones, we had to wait hours, sometimes even days to finally get in touch with someone, and somehow we made it through. Not being available for five minutes is going to be ok too.

When you begin to sit in silence, try to let your thoughts come and go, don't get hung up on them. Don't think about anything that makes you anxious, angry, mad; you get the point. Concentrate on your breathing if you don't want to think about anything. Or just think of things that make you happy. You will start to gain a sense of peace that will hopefully flow into the rest of your crazy day. Although you're going to lose 5 minutes of time you will gain so much by doing this.

CHALLENGE

Sit in silence for five minutes for the next 5 days.

Use the space below to write out any clarity you discovered or any thoughts on this chapter. Feel free to continue the challenge longer, there's no limit to time or number of days to do this. Enjoy!

chapter twenty-four

BEING ALONE

> *"Learn to be alone and like it.*
> *There is nothing more freeing and empowering*
> *than liking your own company."*
>
> – Mandy Hale

Fifteen years ago I would not have agreed with this quote. I rarely liked to be alone. I couldn't sit in a room without a tv or music on. Silence was not only deafening to me, it was unbearable! I preferred large crowds to small company. I wanted to be where the action was! I was bored to tears if I didn't have plans to do something several nights a week. Fast forward to the present. I not only agree with this quote, I totally get it. Don't get me wrong, I still like to go out and I definitely enjoy a good party and catching up with people. I'm certainly not a hermit by any means, but I can honestly say now, I do enjoy my own company.

It is so freeing and empowering to enjoy being alone with yourself. For those of you who don't like being alone—who are a bit like I was 15 years ago— I encourage you to stretch your mind and try to understand why. What is it about being alone you don't like? Why the discomfort? Having been there, I think I know what it might be. I depended on others for my happiness. If I was alone, there was no one there to make me happy. Well, there was ME, but what I didn't realize back then was I hold the key to my happiness. And, by relying on others to bring happiness to me, by avoiding being alone at all costs, I was giving my power away to others rather than developing me. I didn't even know this was what I was doing. I was subconsciously thinking if I have to be alone, I won't be happy, so I better make plans with "whoever" because then I'll be ok. Do you comprehend how I was literally depending on someone else to make me happy?

Do you ever do this? Because maybe, just maybe, if you don't like to be alone, you do this too. If you're the type of person who doesn't like to be alone at all, if you can't stand the thought of a Saturday or Sunday afternoon with no plans and no one around, I encourage you to think about why. What are you making being alone mean? Are you making it mean you've been rejected by others? Try to get to the bottom of your thoughts about being alone.

And just for the record, it's not healthy to be alone all the time. I consider myself an extrovert and I truly do enjoy other peoples' company. I enjoy being married and I feel blessed to have wonderful family and friends. But, even as I type this, I'm alone in our house. Our dog Karma is sitting next to me but my husband is out for the evening. And, I'm ok. I don't feel the need to call anyone to talk, or watch a TV show, or even listen to music right now. I'm just enjoying the peace and quiet of our home and my own company.

CHALLENGE

It depends on if you already enjoy your own company or not. If you do—Kudos to you and I hope you get to enjoy some alone time soon. But, if you don't like to be alone, if being alone makes you uncomfortable, try to figure out why. And if you can—the next time you have some alone time, think about some things you like about yourself because if you can do this, you may start to enjoy your own company.

Use the following space to write down your thoughts on this chapter.

chapter twenty-five

LISTEN AND SILENT

> *"Listen & Silent*
> *are spelled with the same letters.*
> *Think about it."*
>
> – Nikki Sharp

Take the time and think about what each word means. When we listen to someone, we need to be silent in order to truly hear them. But are we? How often do you interrupt someone who is talking, either to prove a point or to tell them something you want to add to the story they're telling? Maybe you're afraid if you wait until they are done talking, you'll forget what you wanted to say. Or maybe you can't help yourself, you just have to open up your mouth and talk.

If we are totally being attentive and listening to someone, we shouldn't be conjuring up what we are going to say next, but we do so out of habit. Because our brains are on autopilot most of the time, when someone is talking we immediately start thinking about how we are going to respond. And an important point to understand is, until they are finished, we have no idea if what we are about to respond with is even relevant to what they are talking about. For example your co-worker could be talking about your boss and how frustrated he is about something that happened at work recently. You immediately jump in before he is finished— telling him how you had a similar situation and this is how you handled it. You think you're helping him by providing a solution, right? You think you're being a good friend—maybe even giving yourself a silent pat on the back for letting him know how you handled a similar situation with success. But if you heard him out to the end, if you didn't jump in with your story, maybe what he wanted to tell you was how he handled it and he felt good about it. Maybe all he wanted was for you to remark "that's awesome, I'm glad you worked it out." Because you jumped in with your story you put the focus on you. I think as adults we do this to children a lot without even realizing it. I know we do it to other people in our life too, we assume that we know what they are going to say and we butt in before they finish.

We should be concentrating on what they are saying, not how we are going to respond. And, let me add I'm just as guilty of doing this as the next person and I realize I need to improve on my listening and staying silent skills too. I'm aware of it and I'm hoping this quote makes you aware if you do this too.

One point I want you to be clear on is I'm not saying you don't share your experiences and you just stay silent all the time. What I'm trying to get you to think about, to stretch your mind and think about, is when someone is talking can you just stay SILENT while they are talking and LISTEN? Can you hold your response till they are done? Can you make the conversation like a tennis match where the ball is always on one side or the other; it's never on both sides at once? The person who has the ball on their side sends the ball to the other side and the other person has to wait for it to get to their side before they can send it back.

CHALLENGE

The next time you are having a conversation
and you have the urge to interrupt the person talking,
think about the tennis match example above
and whether you have the ball before you respond.
Remember, we have two ears and one mouth,
this may not be an accidental design.

Use the following space to write down your thoughts on this chapter.

chapter twenty-six

THE POWER OF SILENCE

> *"Silence is so much more powerful than having the last word."*
>
> \- Annette Q

I find just saying this quote powerful. But I'm sure there are some of you who would disagree. Some people feel that if we are quiet, if we walk away from an argument or conversation that is heated, we are being submissive. Or, they believe it shows we're being weak, or it will look like we're too afraid to speak our mind. I used to think that way. I used to argue my point till I was almost blue in the face. If I felt an injustice then I was going to right the wrong and I would almost gloat over having the last word. "I showed them" I thought to myself, or did I?

When I look back at the times when I did this, I see now it was all about my ego. (See Chapter 8 for more about the ego) I let my ego take over and it had to have the last word. It couldn't bear to let someone else say something I didn't agree with without commenting back. It just wouldn't be right, or so I thought. But then I learned the magic and power of silence. If we can put our ego aside and instead really think about whether we should or need to have the last word in a situation, it can be so freeing. To choose NOT to have the last word, to remain silent—is for me now even better than having the last word.

Think about it. Is it really worth your energy to have the last word? If you are trying to reason with people that are unreasonable then perhaps not. No matter what you say there's a strong chance they just might not "get it". Why get all riled up and let them upset you? Why give them that power? Not everyone has to agree with us. They can think what they want and you can think what you want. I believe it's best to get over the "I'm right and you're wrong" mentality many of us at times struggle with including yours truly. Because when I do think this, I immediately now know it's my ego that thinks this way. Start stretching your mind and think about whether your ego gets the best of you at times. Do you have to be right, even if it's the littlest of things? Do you think being silent is a sign of weakness? Our ego is not always acting in our best interest and it is not always looking out for our health.

But how can being silent be healthy you may be wondering. Or you may be thinking how about what I want to say, why should I remain silent? Well, I'm not advocating you let others walk all over you, I'm not inferring you sit back and allow yourself to be bullied. But, to choose silence over an argument, is in my opinion healthy if—and here's the big IF, IF you can be silent AND be at peace with being silent. This means not stewing about being silent. It means choosing silence because you know that by not saying anything you are holding the Power. When we can walk away without saying a word, (I call it "Being a Bobble Head") and nod our head but not say a word, because inside we know it's not worth our energy; that's healthy. If you are silent however and are stewing inside about being silent; that is not healthy.

If you disagree with this quote, think about why. What

is it about being silent that upsets you? It may be interesting to write those thoughts down and I've provided some space below to do so. Do you look at silence as a weakness? Was there someone in your past who was silent and you felt they were weak? You may uncover and learn more by taking the time to write out your thoughts on this topic.

CHALLENGE

For this week try at least once,
when you find you want to have the last word
in a discussion, when your ego wants you
to have the last word; remain silent instead.
Use your Power and choose to do this.
Don't consider yourself weak, but instead realize
you are remaining silent because you are strong.

Do you agree with the statement "Silence is much more powerful than having the last word"? Why or why not?

chapter twenty-seven

WHAT IS THIS TRYING TO TEACH ME?

"When you replace 'why is this happening to me' with 'what is this trying to teach me?' everything shifts."

- David Avocdo Wolfe

Interesting concept, isn't it? It even has our challenge right in it. But before we get to the challenge for this chapter, let's really stop and think about the possibility of doing this. Of replacing "why is this happening to me" with "what is this trying to teach me"?

Let's stretch our minds with a few warm up questions. How often do you say out loud, or think to yourself "why is this happening to me"? And by the way, it can be any version of these words. "I can't believe this is happening again" you may tell yourself or "are you kidding me?" Some of you may shout or think periodically WTF , we all know that acronym right? How often do you text a friend WTF? Seriously though, throughout your day, throughout a typical week in your life, how many times do you think or say something like this and then not give it another thought? We all do this, at least on occasion. But have you ever noticed whatever happened that made you think or say this often comes up again and again in other circumstances? We may say it, or think it, and then when we don't give it a second thought, it repeats itself in a different form in our lives. Why does this keep happening? If you truly want to know why something keeps happening and how to stop the cyclical pattern, you need to look within; you have to give it a second thought. At times like these you could benefit by asking yourself "what is this trying to teach me?".

We often repeat similar patterns in areas of our life until we learn a lesson from them. Have you ever ended a bad relationship only to be in another relationship that at first appeared different but eventually you started noticing the similarities? An example would be you just got out of a bad relationship with Brian. Then you begin a new relationship with Brad. Soon you realize their similarities and you begin a new relationship with Mark, thinking he is nothing like Brian or Brad. Before long you recognize personality traits among all three that are the same. Instead of being frustrated by these relationships have you ever stopped to ask what is this type of relationship trying to teach me? You could be repeating a bad job pattern too. You may have changed jobs because there were things about the old one you didn't like, and then after you are in your new job for a while; you find yourself still unhappy with your job.

We are creatures of habit, and we are reluctant to look within for answers. It's so much easier to blame others for a relationship gone bad, a job we don't like, pretty much anything in our life we are not satisfied in. When we blame others we take the responsibility off of ourselves. We aren't the problem, they are. We don't have to do anything to fix it, they do. If you want to stop repeating old patterns you need to start asking yourself "what is this trying to teach me?"

CHALLENGE

Notice how often you say or think:
"why is this happening to me?"
Begin today, begin right this moment.
And when you do take notice, remember to replace it with
"what is this trying to teach me?"
Look within, because when you do, "Everything Shifts."

Use the space below to write down any thoughts you have on this chapter.

chapter twenty-eight

FORGIVENESS

(PART 1)

> *"If you can't forgive someone, don't expect others to forgive you."*
>
> – Annette Q

You know I used to hold grudges and remembered the slightest little thing someone did that hurt me. But when I think about it, the only person I hurt when I did this was myself. The person who hurt me because of something they said or did, usually had no clue they hurt me. They could have at the time said they were sorry (an apology I wasn't willing to accept) or they didn't apologize. In either scenario they probably didn't give another thought about it. I, however, usually spent hours going over in my head what happened and often telling other people what they did, which now seems ridiculous but at the time seemed totally appropriate and justified to me.

Let's face it, we all have hurt people and not even known it. So why are you still unwilling to forgive someone? Is there a magical amount of time we need to wait before we forgive someone? Once that time has passed can we then say "Ok, now I forgive you"?

What about forgiveness for big things. Perhaps there is someone in your life, a family member, a friend, a co-worker, who you feel did something that you just can't seem to forgive them for. I want you to think hard about why you can't forgive them. Was your ego hurt? Did they betray your trust? Whatever reason it may be, is it really unforgivable? What in your mind is an unforgivable offense?

How do you feel not forgiving someone? When I ask this question I'm not referring to if you feel justified in not forgiving them. What I'm referring to is how does your body feel? Do you tense up when you tell someone about what happened? Does it cause you anger to even think about it? If it does, this is why forgiveness is for us. It's not good to have a war raging inside of us. It's not healthy. It provides zero benefit for your mental or physical health.

I'm sure this subject and my insight may have touched a nerve with some people and to that I am going to say "I'm sorry, please forgive me". But just think about this—Forgiveness is Forgiveness. Do we need to have a scale to determine what amount of hurt is needed before something is unforgivable? Anyone is worthy of forgiveness. We all want to be forgiven when someone is mad at us, so why should anyone forgive us, if we refuse to do the same for someone else? Think about this for more than five minutes.

CHALLENGE

Use the space below to right down people in your life you have not forgiven. They could be people you need to forgive for simply being themselves. Maybe their personality disagrees with yours and they always tick you off. Whatever the reason, list their names below. Once you have the list, think some more and try to recall if you ever did anything to hurt them and if they forgave you. And, even if you never hurt them, think about forgiving them anyway—not for them—but for YOU!

chapter twenty-nine

FORGIVENESS

(PART 2)

> *"When we forgive we heal,*
> *and when we let go we grow."*
>
> – Author Unknown

This chapter is also about forgiveness but it touches more on the benefits of forgiveness. I'm going to ask you to look back at people in your life you have forgiven and reflect on if you have really forgiven them. Maybe you have forgiven them but you still every once in a while will bring up, either to yourself or to others, what wrong you feel was done by the person to you. To your credit you may even remark "but I've moved on, I've forgiven them" but here's the mind yoga exercise to think about, if you really moved on why bring it up at all, why can't you let it go? And another question to consider is: What's the upside of forgiving but not forgetting?

I feel we sometimes think if we forgive someone, they'll do whatever it was that we forgave them for again. And, we're afraid we'll look like a fool. So we carry around resentments and we keep thinking about the wrong that someone else did to us. We let it become part of our story. We may tell others about it. We may rehash it in our minds a thousand times over and over and over. We think by forgiving we are showing a weakness when in actuality it's harder to forgive. "Why do I have to be the bigger person and forgive?" you may say to anyone who suggests you forgive someone else. Because that's the only way you'll heal is the answer.

So forgiveness is first, but now let's talk about letting go. Another thing to think about the next time you don't want to let it go, when you say you've forgiven someone but you choose not to forget what they did; is the fact that you have no control over whether they will do it again or not. You only have control over whether you choose to forgive them again. If we forgive, not forgetting doesn't stop the person from ever doing it again—it only stops You—it stops you from growing.

Don't get me wrong—forgiveness is great and I commend anyone who can do this because it is by forgiving we heal from our wounds. But it's also only when we can let it go, just like the quote says, that we grow. Continue stretching your mind and really think about this, you can't grow if you're holding on to something. I like to use an example of a baby learning to walk to get people to understand this. If a baby continues to hold on to their parents hands or the coffee table or whatever they are holding on to before they finally let go and take those first steps, they would never learn to walk. You can't move forward if you're holding on to the past. We put our car in drive, neutral or reverse. Our mind is similar; we can be thinking thoughts of where we're going, drive, or where we've been, reverse. It's too bad our minds are rarely in neutral or still. By forgiving we are in neutral. It's better than reverse but we're kind of at a stalemate. By letting go we're moving forward. We're putting our car in drive - we'll go forward and move on.

When we've forgiven but still have not let go, we are (in our mind) holding the person who we've forgiven hostage. And I say in our mind because really if you think about it the person we're holding hostage by not letting go is ourselves. It's you, not them, that keeps reliving the situation that you forgave them from in the first place. That's why or rather how we know forgiveness is not for the other person, it's for our own peace of mind.

CHALLENGE

Think about if there are any people in your life you've forgiven but you're still holding on to the story, you're still reliving the wrong. Take a deep breath and Let It Go...and Grow!

Use the space below to write down any thoughts on this chapter.

chapter thirty

LOVE

"Love people for who they are and not who you want them to be."

- Carolyn Hax

So much easier said than done right? We love many different people in our lives, and we love them each in a different way. We love our parents, our siblings, our friends, our spouse or significant other, our children. But do we truly love them for who they are or are we consciously or subconsciously trying to change them? Think about that. Do some mind yoga with this question: is there anyone you love simply for who they are? If you do, you're very lucky and so are they. That is called unconditional love, love without any conditions or expectations. Unconditional love is something our pets give us all the time. If you own a pet you know exactly what I'm talking about. Our furry friends are so happy when we get home no matter how long we've been gone.

Now think about who in your life you love like that—someone you love just the way they are—flaws and all. You aren't wishing or trying to change them in any way. You don't subtly try to get them to do something you think would be good for them. Don't pretend you don't know what I'm talking about. We all do this. We try to lead the conversation or we drop subtle hints for them to do something that will make us feel better. It's usually because our thought about them is something along the lines of "I think they need to do X" or "I know they'd be happier if they did Y". We justify it by thinking because we love them, we want what's best for them and we also think we know what's best for them. Maybe they would be happier if they took our advice or did what we say. But...and this is a big But...why can't we love them for who they are and not who we want them to be? Why do we want them to change at all?

We usually want to change someone when our needs are not met. We think if they change, we will be happier. This is what most people believe but it's not them changing that would make us happier, it's our thoughts about them changing that would make us happier. I"ll give you an example, what if something was bothering you about your spouse, they weren't doing something you asked them to do and therefore you weren't happy. Maybe you asked him to change the oil in your car and he wasn't doing it. Then what if you overheard he was buying you a new car for your birthday and was going to surprise you. OK, I bet you'd suddenly be happy. But, follow me here, let's say you then find out whoever told you about the new car had false information. It wasn't true at all. There was no new car for your birthday. Now how would you feel? Would you be back to your old feelings? This should prove to you that it's not whether someone changes or not, but our thought about a person or situation that determines our happiness. You were happy when he didn't change the oil because you thought you were getting a new car! I realize this can be hard to understand but if we are ok with people the way they are, flaws and all, we will be happier. Try it even if it's just for this week. Choosing to love is always a good choice.

CHALLENGE

Think of one person in your life who you love
but who you also nudge at times
to try to change them to fit your needs.
For one week try to just love them for who they are.
Can you do that? Can you talk with them
and enjoy your conversation, their company
and appreciate them for who they are?
Can you not once mention something you think
they should be doing or try to correct them in any way?
Love them for who they are!

Feel free to use space below to take any notes and write down any thoughts you have on this chapter.

chapter thirty-one

MUSIC & MEMORIES

> *"Sometimes it only takes one song to bring back a thousand memories."*
>
> – Author Unknown

I picked this quote for my podcast quote the week my Dad passed away. In the days before I had to travel for his wake and funeral I found myself listening to songs he loved, songs we both loved and they brought back so many wonderful memories. I love music, and I am grateful to have lived in a house where music was played and it was played often.

Growing up we had a big stereo in our family room, it was literally a piece of furniture. It had a place for records to be played and also 8 track tapes. The stereo was enormous and it sat in front of our bay window. Between my parents' music and my older siblings' music, I rarely got to listen to what I wanted to, but I did learn to appreciate all sorts of music. From Frank Sinatra and the Supremes, to Earth Wind and Fire and Chicago, we had records and tapes of these artists and many more and we played them all the time. And, what I find so interesting, is how we can hear a song and immediately be taken back in time. You hear the tune and literally you feel like you are back in the moment when that song was popular. It's because of our thoughts about the song. As I've mentioned numerous times before, our thoughts create our feelings and so when we hear the song whatever we are thinking about it, whatever memory it triggers, brings up our emotions associated with it.

Tom Dexter, who I mention in my dedication, told me once every human emotion that has ever been felt is expressed in a song. He said that someone at some point had the exact emotion as you and wrote a song about it. That's pretty wild to think about, but it could be true. And I'm in awe over the people who write music, what a gift. And I'm even more in awe of people who can sing because that is one talent I did not receive. I so wish I could carry a tune, but not being able to doesn't stop me from driving down the highway singing at the top of my lungs when no one else can hear me.

So what songs bring back memories for you? What song can you listen to and never get tired of? What song makes you laugh thinking of times you shared with others listening to it or singing along with it? What song have you sat and listened to all by yourself and maybe even cried?

The night I found out my Dad passed away I sat by candlelight out on our screen porch and listened to Frank Sinatra, his favorite singer. "My Way" was the first song which came on when I turned on my Pandora app. "My Way" is a classic and the lyrics are reflective and powerful. I encourage you to google them if you don't know them. Anyway, "My Way" was my Dad's theme song so to speak and it brought back a thousand memories for me. I will always think of my Dad when I hear that song. And I'll be forever grateful he taught me to appreciate music.

CHALLENGE

Let your mind go back in time
and enjoy listening to music you haven't heard in years.
Think of songs that bring back thousands of memories,
memories you don't ever want to forget.
Remember: "Sometimes It Only Takes One Song
to Bring Back a Thousand Memories".
What Memory do you want to Remember?
Play that Song!

Think about and list below, songs that have special meaning to you. If you had to pick 10 songs to be on your song list for Life, what songs would make the list and why?

My 10 All Time Favorite Songs:

1. ______________________________

____

____

____

2. ______________________________

____

____

____

3. ______________________________

____

____

____

4. ______________________________

5.

6.

7.

8.

9.

10.

chapter thirty-two

ABUNDANCE

> *"We don't create abundance.*
> *Abundance is always present.*
> *We create limitations."*
>
> – Arnold Patent

Abundance is defined by The American Heritage Dictionary as "a great or plentiful amount, a condition of being in rich supply." But it's still something we always need to be reminded of even though it is everywhere. Isn't that interesting? Abundance is always present yet we forget and act like it will go away in an instant. We often have a mindset that if someone else gets something we want, we can't have it too. We get jealous, envious and feelings of fear, inadequacy and other negative emotions start to arise in us. If you live life with the mentality that in order to win, someone else has to lose, you don't understand how limiting you are in your thinking. And you don't understand truly what abundance is all about.

So let's stretch our minds and think about abundance. Our world would be so limited, we'd still be living in caves for heavens sake if people didn't believe there was more to have than what they had. People who believed there is something better out there and decided I not only want it, but I can have it and I'm going to go out and get it. The only lack of abundance there is, is in our MINDS. When we think something is limited, then guess what, it is. Why? Because in our mind we are not going to go any further to get it. We've stopped the process of receiving it, by telling ourselves that we can't have it; someone else got there first, or we lost our chance, or the million other excuses (aka limitations) we use. Our mind is so powerful and we believe everything we think. But everything we think is not true. Have you ever worried yourself sick over a thought and then felt instant relief when you realized it wasn't true? That's how we know all our thoughts are not true.

But there is good news. Whatever thoughts you've had in the past about why you couldn't have something, they are all just limitations you came up with in your mind. They aren't all real and they aren't all true. Yes, a few may be actual limitations, but find your way around them. There's more abundance out there. If you wanted a job and didn't get it, it doesn't mean there's no other jobs out there. It means in your mind you limited yourself to that one job. There's a million other jobs out there, don't give up finding the right one because you didn't get the one job you thought was right for you. Think instead that wasn't the job for me and a better one is out there and I'm going to get it! But aren't we supposed to be happy with what we have? Absolutely. Believing in abundance isn't saying to not be happy with what we have. What believing in abundance means is there is enough for everyone to have what they want to be happy. Once we start believing and living with an abundance mentality, the easier things come to us. The more opportunities come your way. You'll start to realize how limiting you've been with your thoughts.

CHALLENGE

Realize the abundance that is all around you.
Try not to limit yourself in your thinking.
The possibilities and opportunities are endless,
you can have anything you want.

Use the space below to write down everything you want, everything you may have thought in the past was limited and begin to realize the only limit is in your mind.

chapter thirty-three

BEING THANKFUL FOR WHAT WE HAVE

> *"Life is happier when we are thankful for what we have and we do not dwell on what is missing."*
>
> - Annette Q

Many years ago, long before the internet I made a Personalized Christmas Card. On the front of the card it read "I've learned that" and I listed a number of items I had learned that year. One of them was this quote and I think it is relevant now more than ever. We live in a society where people are constantly searching for happiness in the outside world. We want so much, don't we? And, we think once we get what we want we will be happy. Some of us may want a bigger house, some a new job, and others of us may want more money. We dwell on what is missing in our lives and we make our happiness contingent on if we get it or not. And then, as is often the case, we get it and it still doesn't make us happy.

There's a lyric in the Train song "Calling All Angels" which really brings the point of looking for happiness in outside things and being still unhappy once we get it home. The lyric is "In a world where what we want is only what we want until it's ours". Take out your mental mat and think about that. Why is this? It's because true happiness comes from within. I know, I know, it sounds so cliche. We hear this all the time, but guess what? It's TRUE. You can live in that big house that you wanted for so long and finally got, but unless you are happy with yourself you are still not going to be happy for long. You may have temporary happiness upon getting it, but it won't last. Have you ever wanted something so bad and when you did finally get it, you weren't quite as excited as you thought you'd be? That's both reassurance and proof that happiness from outside sources is temporary. We can be told this; we can know this; and we can believe this; but how do we really begin to live this? By remembering if we are thankful for what we have and we don't dwell on what is missing in our lives, we can begin to really be happy. Gratitude is a great way to bring happiness into our lives. You can get rich quick by counting your blessings.

By the way, it's ok to want things, just don't make your happiness contingent on getting them. Here's an example, when I recorded my podcast on this quote I wanted (and I knew I'd have someday) a certain brand of car. I loved the look of it and I knew I'd love driving it. But at the time I was perfectly happy with the car I had. In fact, I loved the car I had; it was over 6 years old and had a ton of miles, but I loved it. The other car I knew I'd have eventually, I didn't need it to be happy. Ironically I received the very car I was willing to wait for about 3 months after my podcast aired. My car needed a lot of work when I took it in for winter maintenance and by a twist of fate I did receive it and Love it!

And I'll end this chapter on a funny note: On Facebook recently somebody wrote: "I've found the key to happiness.

Stay away from assholes". Although I did find humor in that statement, it's still assuming our happiness is contingent on others. The key to happiness isn't staying away from people who bother you, the key is to learn to be happy with yourself and not let others upset you. And when you can do that, when you can be happy in spite of who may be around and be happy with what you have right now, you are on your way to learning inner happiness.

Remember: "Life is happier when we are thankful for what we have and we do not dwell on what is missing"

CHALLENGE

Start to be aware and thankful for
what and who you have in your life
and not dwell on what is missing.
When you notice yourself thinking or saying
anything similar to "I wish I had...whatever"
try to think right away of something in your life
you're thankful for. Write it down if it helps.
Make a list of things you're thankful for if you want to.
And hopefully this will get you to realize you can
be happy with what you have. Because true happiness
cannot be bought and it doesn't involve anyone else.

Use the space below to list some things you are Thankful for in your life right now.

____

____

____

chapter thirty-four

GIVING THANKS

> *"We don't need more to be thankful for, we need to be thankful more."*
>
> – Carlos Castaneda

It's easy to agree with this quote. But, how often do you stop and think about all you have to be thankful for? Let's do some mind yoga and think about this quote. Most of us have more than enough to be thankful for and we don't even realize it. We may think we have to give thanks for big things in our lives, but it's the little things that we should give thanks for too because these little things bring us joy in ways we may not be aware of. I'm going to list a few things we all can be thankful for, things that may not come naturally to the top of your mind when you give thanks. These are things we shouldn't take for granted, but we often do. Please feel free to add as many things as you'd like to this list.

Our five senses — When's the last time you actually thought about the complexity and the magnificence of our five senses? Even if your eyesight or hearing is going bad, the fact that we can fix these things with modern technology is something we should be grateful for. How often do you use your five senses and take them for granted? EVERYDAY is probably the answer. The next time you smell a hot meal in the oven or a scent that you love when you walk in a room; or you feel a soft piece of fabric, hear a bird chirping, taste that piece of your favorite dessert, see a movie that makes you laugh... Say a quick thank you, even if it's just in your head.

Indoor plumbing — Another item we take for granted but is high on my Gratitude list. I can't even imagine having to use an out house in the summer, let alone the winter in the North-east. And the fact that I can turn on a faucet and get hot water almost instantly is a miracle to me. I don't know how it is done, but I give a world of thanks to the engineers who figured out how to make it happen.

Your job — I don't care if you like it or not, give thanks for it. It's paying your bills and it's a reason to get up each morning whether you want to go there or not. If you don't like it, that's ok. Empower yourself to find another one and thank it for showing you what you want in your next job. If you don't have a job, be thankful there are jobs out there. Unemployment in the U.S. is at an all time low, employees are in more demand than ever, be grateful for this too. You have more power than you think in negotiating what you want.

Transfer Stations and Landfills — No, I haven't lost my mind. Please hear me out. What if we had to keep all our garbage ourselves? Gross! I'm so grateful for the County Transfer Station and Recycling Facility. That bill is one I am happy to pay each month. We just bag it up and off it goes. Thank You to all the people who work in this field to make our lives more pleasant.

Music — Can you imagine what the world would be like without music? I am grateful for anyone who ever learned to play an instrument and who put their talents to use so we can reap the benefits. Music can lift our spirits, bring us back to an exact moment in time or a memory we shared. It can make us laugh, or make us cry and it is the universal language we can all relate to. The next time you catch yourself humming a tune or just listening to a song, say a silent thank you. Oh and by the way, you're using one of your 5 senses to hear it too.

Modern technology — Chances are you have some sort of smart phone, iPad or computer, and whether it's the latest version or not, the fact that you even have this technology is something to be thankful for.

Free Podcasts — Another thing we can be grateful for. Unlike paying a cable bill, or a subscription to Netflix or Hulu, most Podcasts are free. I encourage you to check some out and be informed, entertained, or both. Mine is Mind Yoga Quick Quotes with AnnetteQ.

Here's my last, but not my least shout out of Thanks for this chapter:

Our local public and volunteer firefighters and emergency responders — I shudder to think about if my home was on fire and no one was around to respond to a call for help. I say a silent prayer whenever I pass an accident where an ambulance is helping people involved. I'm grateful for all the training you endured and your passion for helping others. I hope I never have to use your services but sleep better at night knowing you are just a phone call away. Thank you for all you do!

CHALLENGE

Use the space below to list things you are thankful for and figure out a way to incorporate gratitude into your life on a daily basis. For example, you can make a list everyday of three things you're grateful for if you want. Or, come up with your own way how to incorporate gratitude into your life. There is no right or wrong way to do this, do what feels right to you. I believe if we learn to be grateful more we'd be angry less. Try it and see.

chapter thirty-five

CLOSED MINDS

> *"Closed minds never open new doors."*
>
> – Annette Q

One of my biggest pet peeves is people with closed minds. Unfortunately, our world is full of them. This quote explains why I feel a closed mind is limiting and not useful. An open mind is crucial if we want to expand our consciousness and live to our best potential. Do you have an open mind or a closed mind? Most people may say they have an open mind, but do they really?

In order to really have an open mind, we need to put our ego aside (there's that ego again) and be able to listen and think if what the other person is saying has validity or not. Listen to their perspective and be open to seeing it from their perspective. Having an open mind also means being willing to change our mind if what they say makes sense. If a family member is giving their opinion on an issue with which you totally disagree with, is your mind open to hearing why they think this way, or do you roll your eyes or cut them off while they are speaking? Or, are you willing to listen to them just to appease them, but deep down inside you have already decided you are sticking with your opinion no matter what they may say? Do you feel angry when a co-worker is trying to explain their point of view? Our bodies tell us a lot about what we are thinking and if you're feeling angry, if you can feel your temperature rising or your heart rate increasing, chances are your mind is not open.

Do you remember asking your parent "why" when you were young and your parent's response was "because I said so"? Parents say no to children for good reason but "because I said so" is not a very mature response to another adult. This is what you are silently saying however when you have a closed mind and you won't even entertain the notion that someone else may have a better idea or a better way of doing something, or a different opinion than yours.

If our Mind is CLOSED, nothing new ever happens. Things continue only as we initially think they should. A closed mind is not merely a closed door; it's a locked door and only you have the key. Opening a door that's been shut for a long time can be scary for some people, what will you find? People often avoid cleaning their attic or garage, or even a closet in their home. It's too daunting to think about, so they leave it as is and just keep throwing stuff in there. Can you see the correlation between a closed mind and a stuffed closet? There's not room for much else and you don't want to open it because that would require you to look at what you've accumulated and deciding what you should throw out because it's no longer useful to you. That takes work and who wants more work to do? Yet have you ever noticed how much better you feel after you've cleaned out a stuffed closet or a closet you avoided cleaning? Well, guess what, the same is true with a closed mind. You can unlock your closed mind. You just have to be willing to do so. And, if and when you do, you will find having an open mind opens up so many possibilities. Abundance is everywhere when we have an Open Mind.

CHALLENGE

Be honest and consider whether you have an Open Mind or not. Maybe you have a "selective" open mind depending on the circumstance. If you have a closed mind in some area of your life, consider opening it. Take time to listen to someone else's viewpoint. Don't form an opinion before you hear them out. Remember: "Closed minds never open new doors."

Use the space below to write down notes and your thoughts on this chapter.

chapter thirty-six

OPEN MINDS WELCOME

"People generally see what they look for, and hear what they listen for."

– Harper Lee
To Kill a Mockingbird

Let's start getting our minds thinking, stretching, and pondering whether we agree with this quote or not. Do you tend to see what you are looking for? If you are always looking on the bright side, that's great and kudos to you. What if a friend tells you something negative about a person before you even meet them? Do you upon introduction to them, start to look for even more traits that are negative?

Let's examine why we do this. One reason may be it's easier to just take someone else's word for something . We don't have to do anything but let them decide for us, but wait a minute, do we really want to do this? Probably not, if you really think about it, but how often do we let a remark made by someone else, about another person make us biased and look for negative things in them to confirm this? More than we realize and more than we'd care to admit, may be the answer for some of us on this question. However, if you are looking for someone to be a jerk you interpret things about them differently than if you were told they were the nicest person on earth.

We probably do this when we respect the person who gave us the negative information about the person in the first place. We should however learn to form our own opinion and not be swayed by what others may think. Just because we may have a different opinion than our friend doesn't mean we still don't respect them.

We see what we want to see with a lot of things, not just with people. It can be a beautiful sunny gorgeous day but if you are looking for an excuse to not go to an outdoor activity you'll exclaim "oh it's too hot out". We want to get out of doing whatever it is so we will use the weather (even if it is beautiful) as our excuse not to participate. We may say it's too hot one day but later in the week it could be the same weather and since we now want to go to an outdoor concert, we think the weather is perfect and we go.

The same is true when we are listening. We hear what we want to hear; we hear what we are listening for. We interpret what others are saying based on what we want it to mean or what we think they mean. It's human nature and don't feel bad if you do this; instead just take notice if you do and decide if you want to continue to do so.

We see and hear what we are looking for when our minds are not open. An open mind is a beautiful thing but we don't even recognize when our own mind is closed.

The next time you form an opinion on something or someone, think about whether you had your mind open or closed before you did so. Was your opinion based off a statement made by someone else and you were looking for confirmation, or was it based on your own open mind? In Mind Yoga; Open Minds are always Welcome!

CHALLENGE

Have an Open Mind
in at least one conversation this week,
one that you already think could be a challenging one.
Try not to have a preconceived opinion of how it will go
or what you may hear. Maybe, just maybe,
you will see or hear it differently.

Use the space below to write down your thoughts on this chapter.

chapter thirty-seven

STAYING IN CONTROL

"Take control instead of losing control."

- Annette Q

What is your first thought on this quote? Is it "I rarely or never lose control"? If it is, good for you! I want you to think about how you interpret "losing control". Some people may interpret it as screaming or yelling, others may interpret it as kicking something or bursting out in tears. Losing control means losing your ability to think and act rationally.

Are there times when you lose the ability to think rationally? Although I'm not proud of it, there's times when I do. We all lose control at times and the reason why we do is because of our feelings, which come from our thoughts. In fact, I have to tell you a funny true story that is a perfect example of someone losing control. I had an old boyfriend who one time missed a putt while we were golfing and he threw his putter in the air causing it to land in the branches of a nearby tree. His thought on missing the putt made him feel enraged and his action from this feeling was flinging his putter in the air. At first I was horrified as he started "losing control" but when his putter stuck in the tree, my horror turned into laughter, which he did not appreciate. I use this example to demonstrate how if we lose our ability to think rationally, we are not going to act rationally. We will lose control. It happens to some of us more than others, but I'm sure everyone has a story or two of how they lost control and wish they had remained in control.

So how do we "Take control"? Well, if we know our actions come from our feelings, which come from our thoughts, the logical solution is to take control of our thoughts.

But how do we do this? We literally have tens of thousands of thoughts each day. Some of you may be thinking there's no way you can control your thoughts, others of you may be thinking you don't have the time or energy to take control of your thoughts. Ok, if you don't want to, that's your choice. But, for those of you who want to try losing control less and taking control more, your next exercise is to think about a time or two when you almost lost control but you stopped yourself. Can you recall anytime when you've done this? Maybe you were about to raise your voice while talking to someone and someone else unexpectedly walked in the same room so you stopped yourself. Maybe when you were younger you were about to swat one of your siblings and your parents walked in the room and you decided against it. How about stopping yourself from blurting out something that you know you shouldn't? Whatever the situation you recalled is, notice how you took control instead of losing control. And, give yourself credit for doing this. You actually stopped yourself from losing control. If you can now continue thinking about the situation where you took control, stretch your mind some more and think about how you felt once you did this. Did you feel better? What was your thought when you took control? What made you stop and what was your thought? That may be a hard one to recall. The thought that made you stop probably had to do with how losing control would not have a good ending. When we lose control we rarely feel good about it. Not that it doesn't feel good to release some negative energy, but if you did it in a bad way, there's usually feelings of remorse afterwards. We can learn how to release some of our negative energy in a positive way. It's not that hard but it takes awareness of when you are about to lose control and very calmly removing yourself from the situation. You could go for a walk, or go for a run. You could go somewhere quiet and write down everything you are thinking and feeling and then tear it all up. You could take that negative energy and clean a room in your house or do anything that keeps you in control while you release some negative energy. And the bonus is you are being productive too.

The Oscar for Best Picture this year went to The Green Book. The movie was phenomenal and is a true story about an accomplished concert pianist who hires an Italian-American bouncer to drive him during his 1962 tour of the South as protection against the racism that he, as an African American, is certain to encounter. The main character, who could have lost control numerous times, was very eloquent and poised. I kept thinking as I was watching it, I can't believe what he had to endure and he never lost his temper. But then I realized the power we give away when we lose control. We let someone else, or a situation get the best of us. And, like I said before, we are rarely ever glad we did. We gain peace by keeping our power.

CHALLENGE

The second you notice when you are about to lose control,
uncover what is your thought right at that moment.
That thought is going to create your feeling,
which will create your action.
Begin to take control
instead of losing control.

Use the space below to write anything down you want to about this chapter.

chapter thirty-eight

CONTROL YOUR MIND

> *"Don't let your mind be*
> *like a runaway train.*
> *Give it a destination and go there!"*
>
> – Annette Q

One of the slides I show people in my workshop, Bootcamp for your Mind, is a cartoon picture of a runaway train. The reason I show this picture is so people have a visual of what their mind looks like without a conductor. Even though there are tracks for it to follow, a trains conductor controls its speed and keeps the train on its tracks. A train doesn't just stay on a straight course to get from point A to point B. It must navigate around curves, and it has to go up and down hills. Without a conductor, it wouldn't be able to get to its destination safely. Its speed would keep increasing and if no one is there to monitor it, it could soon be heading toward a disaster. Do you now understand the correlation between a train and our mind? We are our Minds Conductor. We have the power and the capability to keep our mind on track or allow it to jump off the track.

We have total control of its speed. We navigate it through difficult terrain and smooth terrain. The one thing we can do that a real train conductor can't, is we are able to get our mind back on track whenever it goes off its course.

Start stretching your mind right now and think about how often you let your mind go wild. Do you forget you are the conductor and you DO have control over your mind? I talk in previous chapters how our mind goes on autopilot if we are not aware of what we are thinking. When our mind goes on autopilot, it can become a like a runaway train. But now take a moment and think about where you want to go. What do you want to achieve? You can think about what you want to do today, or you can think about a million other things. Scientists estimate our minds have over 50,000 thoughts a day. We could go crazy trying to control each of those thoughts, but we don't need to. We have unconscious and conscious thoughts. The thought before you raise your hand is an unconscious thought. But what if you start to control a few of your conscious thoughts? Ever find yourself daydreaming, that is an unconscious thought but once you are aware of it, it becomes a conscious thought. If you want to become the conductor of your mind, start becoming aware of some of your thoughts and begin to notice when a thought is picking up speed and is taking off in the wrong direction. You know what I'm referring to; when you start to obsess over something you have no control over and you keep thinking a negative thought again and again. Start by being aware when you are doing this and then begin your new role as conductor of your mind and get your thoughts back on track. What I mean by this is deciding what thoughts you do want to think about. You can have control over your thoughts, please refrain from believing you can't, it's just the way you are. I would say that's just the way you WERE. If you want to change your thoughts, you can. You hold the power to do so, not anyone else.

CHALLENGE

Pretend you are an observer of your thoughts.
As you become more aware of your thoughts,
take one negative thought that is picking up speed
and get it back on track.
Start to become the Conductor of your
Mind and your Life.

Use the space below to write down some of your thoughts. It is helpful to write our thoughts down. This is why journaling is beneficial. By verbalizing our thoughts on paper, we can see how many different thoughts we have and we can choose whether we want to think a thought or not. Ask yourself if any of these thoughts could become like a runaway train and decide if you want to continue the thought or change it before it takes you off course.

chapter thirty-nine

ACCEPTING WHAT WE CANNOT CHANGE

> *"I can't change it,*
> *I can only do my best with it."*
>
> – Karen Macri

My friend said this during a conversation we were having about one of her family members who was a perfectionist and how difficult it was for her to deal with it sometimes. What amazed me was her ability to recognize and accept this fact without blaming or trying to change the person. When I told her this she still made me laugh when she replied "I recognize it but it is still hard to keep my mouth shut".

How do we learn to accept others and stop trying to change them? Well, I believe the first thing we need to do is acknowledge the only person we can change is ourselves. If you don't believe this, if you still want to believe you can change someone and you have to try to change someone, then you are not going to be able to accept the fact you can't. But, if you are now understanding "I can't change it, I can only do my best with it," begin to recognize when you want to change someone. I can't stress this enough, awareness is the first step in finding inner peace. Until we're aware, we are on autopilot and reacting versus responding to anyone and everything around us. And once your'e aware of when you want to change someone, it is up to you to let whatever it is go; let them be who they are. I talked about this also in Chapter 30 and I know it's hard to do. I understand you want what is best for them and maybe you're scared of what will happen if they don't change. Maybe what they won't change about themselves drives you crazy, but you will not find any peace till you can learn to accept them for who they are.

So let's stretch our minds and think about what my friend said and all the people in your life you wish you could change. Seriously, if you had a magic wand and could wave it in front of someone and they would change into the person you want them to be, how many people would you be waving that wand at? Maybe 1, 2, 10, 25? What's the number of people you want to change? I actually don't know my number, but I can tell you if I had a wand that could do that —my arm would be exhausted from waving it around all day long. Or I'll correct myself and say if I had that wand 5 years ago my arm would be exhausted from waving it around all day. I've learned and grown a lot since then, and that's what my hope is for you too.

Even though you don't have a magic wand, how much time do you spend trying to change others? Are there times you find yourself dwelling about how someone reacted to you or a situation long after it happened? Do you realize—and I mean truly realize—you can't change reality so all you are doing is spending time on something out of your control? I'm not sure people fully comprehend this. And it's not because they are unwilling to understand, it's because they truly believe their situation is different. They believe their situation is the exception to the rule, or they have to try to change the person because it is in this person's best interest to change.

Our hearts may be in the right place when we want to change someone or a situation but there's a key ingredient to happiness you need to know and understand. The ONLY person you have control over is You. There was a time when I wanted to control others and I think this was because I felt if I could control them, I'd be happier. Makes sense, right? Well, it does if our happiness is dependent on someone else doing what we want them to do. But, it's so much more freeing to be happy regardless of whether someone does what we want them to do. We can be happy even if someone is not doing what we want them to do. We really can but it takes awareness and work on our part. When we accept the fact that we can't change others, we can accept others for who they are and although their actions may still cause us a little anxiety now and then, (which is because of our thoughts about the situation) we are no longer frustrated with trying to change them. Once we give up having this frustration, we are free to accept them for who they are.

Maybe you disagree with me. I've had clients who were convinced if they could change their spouse they'd be happier and they were determined to do so. Or, they were going to get their boss to see their point of view on something, or get their kids to finally understand the importance of getting good grades—you name it, I've heard countless times the ideas people have had on how they were going to change someone and how much happier everyone would be. But, I've rarely have had someone, like my friend Karen, say what is so obvious and so profound; "I can't change it, I can only do my best with it." I've left some space for you at the end of this chapter to write down the people you want to change and also a space for why. Why is your happiness dependent on them changing? You may find some interesting answers to this question when you start writing down your reasons.

Here's one last question for this chapter—how do you like it when someone is trying to change you? Has anyone ever tried to change something about you and you got upset? The shoe on the other foot doesn't feel so great. Think about that next time you want to change someone else. Acceptance of ourselves and others can bring more peace and joy into our lives.

CHALLENGE

Be aware of when you want someone to change
and instead of trying to change them,
let them be who they are.
Try it once, just to start practicing this
and see if you find some peace. Remember the quote,
repeat this mantra if you need to
"I can't change it, I can only do my best with it".
Learn to start accepting others for who they are.

People I want to Change:

Why do I want to Change Them:

chapter forty

EXCUSES

> *"As we begin the new year let's leave our excuses in last year."*
>
> – Author Unknown

This was the quote for my first podcast of the New Year and I am keeping it for this book because we can replace the years with any timeframe. The quote asks us to stop making excuses and start taking responsibility for our lives. In the next chapter I talk a lot about emotional adulthood. For this chapter you need to know the definition of emotional adulthood, which is taking responsibility for our thoughts, feelings and actions. Once we are in emotional adulthood we stop making excuses.

In order to eliminate using excuses, we first need to recognize how often we make excuses and how often we use others as our excuse. Start stretching your mind and take a moment to think about all the times in the past year, or even the past month, you made an excuse and blamed it on another person. It could be an excuse for things not going right in your life or an excuse why you were late. It doesn't matter what it was for, what matters is if whether you took responsibility for it or you blamed it on someone else. If you don't have the relationship you want with your spouse, your mother, a sibling, a friend, a co-worker; do you blame them? I have talked about forgiveness and often we don't have the relationship we want because we can't forgive. Think about that for a second. Do you use the excuse "I just can't forgive them" as the reason you may not have a good relationship with someone? Are you inferring you don't have a choice? I find it so ironic when people do this, because we all have that choice; we can choose to forgive or we can choose not to, but it's our choice.

What other excuses did you use last year or last month that held you back in some area of your life? If you aren't in the job you want, what excuse did you use for that? If you wanted to lose weight but didn't, what excuse did you use for not losing weight?

Not living where you want to live? What excuse do you use for why this is so? Are you waiting to retire to move to your dream location? It's totally ok if you are, but instead of using your job or anything else as an excuse, why not just admit you're not ready to move to that location now? By doing this you're taking responsibility and not making an excuse for why you are living where you live now. Do you understand when we blame our circumstance on anything other than ourselves, we are not taking responsibility for our lives?

Some of you may be thinking there are times it may sound like you are making an excuse but you are just stating a fact and I agree. If you want to move to a new house but can't afford the house you want, you may say you can't move right now. The fact in this situation is you can't afford the house you want. But if you use your job as your excuse for not being able to afford it, stating it doesn't pay enough for you to buy the house, that is blaming your job. You could take responsibility and say you don't have the money right now for a new house.

Spend some time and think how often your excuse puts the blame on someone else and not yourself. Many of us do this, but if you recognize yourself doing this, realize the minute you blame someone else you give them all the power for your happiness. If you are blaming someone else for why something didn't work out the way you wanted, you are giving them the power to make you happy and you're not taking responsibility for your own happiness. We often make excuses out of habit. At a young age we may have learned to blame things on others and not ourselves because we were afraid of getting in trouble for doing something wrong. Each time we make an excuse, we're moving farther away from what we want and often we don't even know we are doing this. Excuses enable us to avoid taking responsibility of what we usually can control in our lives. If you really want to do something, you can use an excuse or you can make it happen.

CHALLENGE

Start a "No Excuses" journey right now.
Think about what you want to achieve.
What do you want in your life?
Who do you want in your life?
What do you want to be doing a year from now?
Start taking steps towards your goals and your dreams.
And if you start to stumble, don't make an excuse
and give up. Get back up and take responsibility
for what happened and continue moving forward.
Excuses are in the past, we left them behind remember?
They served no useful purpose.

Use the space below to start writing your journey.

chapter forty-one

ATTITUDE & EFFORT

> *"The two things in life*
> *you have total control over*
> *are your attitude and your effort."*
>
> – Billy Cox.

This quote is something we need to remind ourselves of daily. And, it echoes a quote by Charles Swindoll that says, "Life is 10% what happens to me and 90% how I react to it". In a previous office I kept it on the wall of my cubicle and looked at it daily. And, it's so TRUE. We do have control over our attitude and yet we constantly blame others if we are in a bad mood. We do this and don't even know we are doing it. We are subconsciously telling ourselves we do not have control over our own mood. It's important to realize though, it's not their fault, it's OURS. The minute we blame someone else and not take responsibility for our attitude, we are letting them have our Power.

I get it, trust me I do. You think you're in a bad mood because someone ticked you off, or let you down, or whatever. But this is where I need you to stretch your mind and think

—if they didn't do whatever it was that upset you, would you be ok? You may obviously respond "yes" but do you see how their behavior just controlled your mood? Because they did whatever they did, you're now upset. Your thought about what they did is making you feel a certain way. You are therefore letting them control your attitude, not you. We subconsciously think, or you may even admit this "If everyone would just do as I say and act how I want them to act then I'll be happy". And although this may sound nice, it's not realistic So I ask you to go on a journey with me right now and step into reality. We are going to walk through the door from emotional CHILDHOOD into emotional ADULTHOOD. Emotional adulthood is when we start taking responsibility for our thoughts, feeling and actions. In emotional adulthood, you also start taking responsibility for your attitude because you now understand how you have control over your attitude. Any emotion we have is caused by our thoughts. You can change your thought which made you upset or you can be upset and take responsibility for knowing your thought is making you upset.

There are other ways you can try to shift your mood too. One is counting your blessings. Seriously, if you're in a bad mood, start thinking about things you're grateful for. You may be surprised how quickly you forget your bad mood and feel better.

The other trick to improving your mood is to think "and that's ok" after any thought you have that is putting you in a bad mood. Example, "I'm going to be late for this event...and that's ok" or "I'm so mad right now...and that's ok". You may be amazed at how adding those words after any thought can calm us down or put us in a better mood. You and you alone are the only one who can control your attitude.

And what about effort? Our effort we definitely can control and our effort is hard to blame on anyone else. It can be summed up pretty easily: a little effort usually produces little results. Own the amount of effort you put into something.

Don't make excuses why you may not have given your full effort. Maybe it wasn't important enough, and that's ok if it wasn't. Just recognize you have total control over your effort. Not your boss, not your significant other, not your Mom, Dad, dog or kids. You and you alone have control over your attitude and your effort.

CHALLENGE

Start taking responsibility for
your attitude and your efforts.
Own them, don't make excuses or blame others.
Stay in emotional adulthood.

What do you currently blame others for? Do you understand emotional adulthood, why or why not? Use the following space to write down any notes or thoughts you have on this chapter.

chapter forty-two

FEELING ROOTED

"To be rooted is perhaps
the most important and least recognized
need of the human soul."

– Simone Weil

Let's begin this chapter by taking out our mental mats and thinking about this quote from Simone Weil. What does "to be rooted" mean? If you're familiar with yoga as a form of exercise, yoga talks a lot about being rooted. Various poses in yoga encourage you to feel rooted, with tree pose being the most obvious. But throughout a yoga class you're constantly directed into poses which help you find your balance and feel a connection with the earth.

For me, being rooted is about feeling solid and strong. Think about a tree and how the roots of a tree usually go deep into the earth, keeping it from falling over, even in the fiercest of storms. Only when the roots are not solid, when they've been compromised does the tree fall. That's what I feel this quote is about. It's about the benefits and importance of feeling rooted. When we don't feel connected to our soul, we are out of alignment and we show signs of disrespect to ourselves and others. Our roots have weakened and we aren't even aware of it. We suddenly become irritable and annoyed. We may say or do things we will regret later. We often blame and/or criticize ourselves and others. Like a tree without strong roots, we may be subject to falling and we need to strengthen our roots by connecting more to our soul.

When we are off balance, when we don't feel grounded to our core belief system, we often do the opposite of what we need to do to replenish ourselves and get back on solid ground. We substitute taking the time to understand and correct why we are feeling off balance with "mindless busyness". And that's just what it is "mindless" because if we don't think deeply, we don't have to feel deeply. Instead of recognizing what is happening and taking more self care and reflection, we ignore the feelings of being out of balance and we do more destruction to our soul. Examples of this may be taking on an extra project around the house or at work, over committing to help others; anything to take our mind off of what we may be feeling.

Our feelings come from our thoughts. You may think you are ok because you aren't allowing your feelings to get the best of you but if you are avoiding feelings, you will never be at peace with yourself or others. And, they will keep coming back because you have not resolved those feelings. Do you ever get yourself in a situation that is similar to one before, even though you swore you would never allow it to happen again? This could be because you didn't really deal with the feelings from the first situation. Patterns repeat themselves for a reason. Until we are willing to break a pattern it comes back. And let me explain what I mean when I say this. It takes more than just declaring it will never happen again to break a pattern. It's figuring out what happened, examining our part in why it happened and then working on ourselves so it doesn't happen again. It's great to recognize you don't want something to happen again, but just proclaiming that you're not going to allow it anymore won't stop it from happening again.

If you are continuously in relationships where you're unhappy, is it really the other person's fault all the time? I've had clients tell me they're tired of doing what their significant other wants to do all the time but when I ask them if they ever expressed to them what they want to do they say no. We then work on why they don't have a voice in the relationship and we work on breaking that pattern so they can have a voice and feel more in control of their life.

To feel rooted we need to know our core values: what do we believe in? Our decisions can then be based on these core values. Here's an example in case you are confused. You believe spending quality time with your spouse is important to a healthy marriage. But, you look back over the last month and you had little quality time. So you have to make some choices if it's truly important to you. Any upcoming decisions on ways to spend your free time should then be based on whether it takes away from quality time with your spouse. If you haven't spent any time together and someone calls to ask you to go see a movie you've been wanting to see, maybe you should decline and make plans with your spouse. If we say yes to everyone else, and no to doing things with our spouse, then we aren't going to feel rooted in our marriage.

Think about what's important to you and if your decisions accurate reflect what you want. When our decisions contradict our values is when we usually feel off-balance. We're often unaware of this. That is why feeling rooted is an unrecognized need. Start strengthening your roots, one decision at a time.

CHALLENGE

Think about the quote "To be Rooted is Perhaps the Most Important and Least Recognized Need of the Human Soul" and write down what it means to you. Take that small step and once you know what it means to you, try to honor it by recognizing when you don't feel rooted or what triggers you and sets you off-balance. Recognize your need to feel rooted.

Use the following space to write down your thoughts on this chapter.

chapter forty-three

TAKING CHARGE OF YOUR DAY

"Either you run the day or the day runs you."

- Jim Rohn

Do you make a To Do list every day? And if you do, do you just have it in your head or do you write it down? Maybe you don't make one every day but you make one on occasion. There's no right or wrong answer to any question I ask, but if you are not a "To Do" list type of person, stretch your mind and answer this question: if you don't have a plan for the day, how do you get what you want to accomplish for the day done? I don't mean to sound sarcastic; I am asking you this to get you to uncover whether you are running your day or whether you are letting the day run you. Do you feel in control of your day, or not? When you don't, you are letting the day run you.

It's important to have downtime and maybe there are days where we don't have anything specific we want to accomplish. Days when we just want to, and need to relax. I'm not referring to those days in this chapter. But we all have plenty of days when we do need to get things done and we still let the day run us. It's only logical if you don't take charge and run your day, the day is going to run you. You are going to be at the whim of every circumstance and person around you and you probably won't get much done that you wanted to do.

I'm a big list maker. I have a list for work and a list for my personal life everyday and I'm not encouraging you to go to the extreme that I do. There are also plenty of days when I don't get everything on my list done. But think about this: if you know a few things you want to get done for the day, why not write them down and then you can use the list as a way to make decisions for the day? This list will help you "run the day" versus "the day running you".

How? This might sound obvious to some of you but appease me a bit and follow this example. Let's say you had a list and on your list were 3 things you wanted to accomplish; get to the dry cleaners; go to the bank for something and return a blouse. So you leave your house and head for the bank and you get a call from a friend who wants to meet for coffee. You immediately say sure and meet her before going to the bank. The moment you let that call take over what you were going to do is the moment you start letting the day run you. Do you see how quickly this can happen?

So how can you run the day in this circumstance? Instead of saying sure and going to meet her, already putting one of your To Do list items on hold, why not tell your friend "I'd love to, I just have to get to the bank first, let's meet in an hour." Now some of you may do exactly that, which is commendable. Yet I've had people tell me they are hesitant to say this because what if their friend couldn't meet in an hour and they really wanted to see them? My response is "did you even ask?" You know you have to get to the bank, so why not ask if they can meet a little later so you can get what you need done; why not put yourself first? There's no harm in meeting your friend for coffee and I'm not suggesting you start becoming a methodical machine that is not flexible. But do you see how if we are in control of our day versus the day controlling us it may be beneficial? We will get more done if we are in control of our day. We get distractions all day long. We can always find ways to let the day run us. Have you ever said, "I don't know where the day went?" Bingo—this is why. We let little distractions get in the way of what we want or need to do. Remember, either you run the day or the day runs you. The choice is yours to make.

I use a system on my To Do list using the acronym WIN. I don't remember who told me about it or who developed it but it stands for What's Important Now. After I finish my list I write a "W" next to the first item I want to get done, an "I" next to the second and a "N" next to the 3rd item. These are now the top 3 things I need to get done and I use this system to prioritize my list. It may not be a system you want to use but it could help plan your day.

CHALLENGE

If you're not a list maker, take baby steps and use one for one day. Make a list of a few things you want to accomplish and base your decisions on getting those items done. You may like it so much you do it the next day. You may hate it and never want to do it again; and that's ok too. Feel free to use the space below to make your list.

TO DO LIST:

___

___

___

___

chapter forty-four

THE PAST

> *"We are products of our past, but we don't need to be prisoners of it."*
>
> – Rick Warren
>
> The Purpose Driven Life

I like this quote for a lot of reasons but here are my top 3:

1. It reminds us how we are in control of our lives.
2. It expresses how we can and should move on from our past.
3. It acknowledges the prison we hold ourselves in by continuing to look backwards.

Let's talk about the past; it's over, right? Can we agree the past is over and all we have now is the present and the future? Good, now I want you to think about how many times you use your past as an excuse for how you are now. Or, how many times you use your past as an excuse for a situation you are in now. If you're in turmoil over something or unhappy about something, whether it be your relationship status, your job, your home life, your fear of doing something, anything at all, do you find yourself commenting (or even thinking) "well that's how I grew up"? Do you still talk about the time your Mom, Dad, Brother, Sister, Aunt, Uncle or whoever did something that was damaging to you in some way and it hurt your feelings? How often do you relive this incident in your mind or by telling the story to others? I realize I just asked you a lot of questions but I need you to stretch your mind, and to have an open mind, while I ask a few more. Don't get defensive and if you really want to practice some mind yoga answer these questions: If something in your past was so bad, why do you want to keep it fresh in your mind? Why keep yourself in a mental prison by revisiting it? I get it, you were hurt and I'm not diminishing your hurt but you don't have to continue the hurt. Do you think by not giving it up you're honoring yourself because if you really think about it, you're not. By allowing yourself to continue being affected by it, you're doing more damage than good to yourself.

You are the only one who can control how you look at the situation now. You can continue to think about it, talk about it and keep it fresh in your consciousness or you can realize although we are all products of our past, our past does not have to define who we are now. We can choose to escape the prison of past disappointments, regrets, unfortunate circumstances and emotional hurt and make our future what we want it to be.

You know it's ironic because recently I realized I was holding on to an event from my past. I was talking with another coach and telling her something that happened and she pointed out to me that I was retelling a story from my past and making it define me. I started to laugh because I had already taken some notes on this quote, about how damaging telling old stories to ourselves can be, and I was doing exactly that to myself. I'm telling you this so you realize that although I'm a Life Coach, I am human too. Once when I was upset a friend remarked "you're a life coach, you shouldn't be upset". I never realized till then that is a misperception people may have so let me clarify right now,

I do get upset over things. It would be unrealistic to never get upset. The difference now is I'm much more aware of why I may be upset and I know how to coach myself through a thought more easily than the next person. But just to be clear, I have to practice everything I talk about on me too. The challenge I give you, I also give to myself. Why? Because as I keep mentioning, our minds go on autopilot and old bad habits resurface when we are not aware of how our thoughts truly create our feelings.

CHALLENGE

Let Go of old stories about your past that no longer serve you. When you find yourself bringing up a story from your past as an excuse for how you are now, STOP—Let it Go. Don't use that as your excuse anymore. Your only excuse is YOU not wanting to let it go. You may not even realize you're doing it, but try to catch yourself next time and Let it Go. Move forward. Take responsibility for your thoughts, your feelings and your actions by not holding yourself in a mental prison. You hold the key to get out. Take the key and let yourself be Free!

What stories from your past are you willing to let go? Use the space below to write down any notes or thoughts you have on this chapter.

____

____

____

chapter forty-five

BEING PRESENT

> *"Be where you are."*
>
> - Karen Keis

This quote is something a friend of mine said to me last summer. Let me give you a little background on why she said it. We're both lucky enough to live in beautiful Saratoga Springs NY and if you know anything about Saratoga you know it is a horse town and the Thoroughbred Race Track is a big attraction for six weeks every summer. We were at the Track having breakfast one Sunday morning watching the beautiful horses get their morning workout in before the races. There were six of us in our group and as we were talking with each other we, one by one, started reaching for our phones for various reasons. Some of us were checking the weather for the day, some of us were checking text messages as they dinged on our phone, some of us were on google trying to get answers to questions we had about the Tracks history and one of us (OK this one I have to admit was me) was trying to order a top I wanted because I was afraid I'd forget to order it by the time I got home.

Suddenly Karen said in a very stern voice: "Hey...put your phones down and be where you are". "Be Where You Are" hit me like a glass of cold water being thrown in my face. I realized she was absolutely right. Here I was on my phone instead of observing the dew coming off the grass, the horses galloping by, and the commentator telling us interesting facts about what was going on. There were all sorts of things I was missing because I had my head in my phone. You know that statement "you've got your head up your ass"? Well, these days we should change it to "You got your head in your phone".

Just because we can look up anything we want in a nano second doesn't mean we have to or that we should. Especially if we are in the company of others. Our phones have become such a part of our lives, part of our communication, that we often don't think twice about using them in the middle of conversations, at business meetings, even as we're grocery shopping.

A few weeks ago I thought a woman in the produce section of the grocery store was nuts. She appeared to be yelling at the tomatoes, then I thought maybe there was a child I couldn't see with whom she was upset. I finally realized she was screaming at someone on her cell phone as she picked out her vegetables. I later saw (or rather heard) her in the dairy aisle and she was still at it, screeching at someone on her phone and shopping like she was the only person in the store. Our town used to have a sandwich shop that had a sign on the door which read "We appreciate your business, but we don't want to know your business. Please refrain from being on your phone". I loved this sign. And I loved my friend Karen pointing out to me recently "Be Where You Are".

How often are you not fully present because you are looking up something on your phone? Does anyone remember before cell phones? Do you ever just drive down the road and look at the landscape around you anymore? Do you ever go for a walk and leave your cell phone at home? I'm just as guilty as the next person, I bring my phone pretty much everywhere these days, and since I'm not a brain surgeon I'm pretty sure no one needs to get in touch with me to save a life. If I missed a call and was to call back in 1/2 hour or even a few hours it wouldn't be detrimental to anyone's health. Dependency on our phones has become a bad habit for most of us. We could all learn to look at them less and be in the moment more and that would benefit everyone in our lives.

CHALLENGE

"Be Where You Are" and notice when you are not.
And when you're not, try to put your phone down and
"Be Where You Are".
What is your biggest fear about
missing a call on your cell phone?
Do you feel you spend too much time checking your phone?
Could you benefit from being away from it
for an hour or two each day?
What would you do with the time?

Use the space below to answer these questions and for your thoughts on this chapter.

chapter forty-six

THE PRESENT MOMENT

> *"Become friends with the present moment."*
>
> – Eckhart Tolle

This quote was used in yoga class by our instructor and very good friend of mine, Judy Pawlick. It stuck in my mind, throughout our practice that day and I thought it would provide some great mind stretching exercises.

First mind-stretching question: how often are your thoughts about things either in the past or coming up in the future? Throughout your day, when you catch yourself focusing on a thought, does it have to do with something that happened already, or does it have to do with something you are anticipating happening in the future? Here's another question: how often are your thoughts about enjoying the moment you're in? If you are like most people your thoughts are more about the past or future than the present moment.

We live in a society of multi-tasking and instant gratification. We are either living in the past, or planning for our future. And by the way, don't get me wrong, I think planning for your future is a very important thing to do. But, when we are not living in the present moment and a majority of our thoughts are either about the past or the future, we are not fully enjoying where we are now. We are so caught up in planning our future we are forgetting to enjoy the moment we are in. Try to remember and understand this moment is never going to happen again. You can't get it back.

Are there times in your past you didn't enjoy as much as you could because you couldn't wait for your life to move on—for something in the future? When I was younger I had summer jobs but I couldn't wait until I finished college to get a full time job and make more money. I wanted to buy my own car, spend money on clothes , and have money to spend however I decided to spend it. I thought making more money was the end all to my happiness. When I started my first full time job however, I remember wishing I enjoyed my summer jobs more. I had great summer jobs, and I had a lot of fun, but I don't think at the time my mindset was telling me to just enjoy the time in my life for what it was. My mindset was on my future self.

So how do we make friends with our present moment? I think the first thing we need to do is accept where we are now. If it's not where you want to be, that's ok. Know you don't have to stay here, but if you are working so hard for something you want in the future that you're not at peace with where you are now, you're missing out on your own happiness right now. You're actually telling yourself not to be happy until something else happens and you're sabotaging your happiness today. But, if we can accept where we are, even if it's not where we ultimately want to be, we can become friends with our present moment. We may even find things about the present moment we like.

A few years ago I was going through a very challenging time in my life and I had to take a miserable trip which required me to drive 5 hours in the dead of winter to a place I didn't want to be. Before I left a friend remarked to me that they hoped I had a good time and I remember responding "I'll make it a good time". I think that is when I realized I had to start making friends with the present moment because the alternative was to not enjoy it, and that's no fun.

Are you not at your goal weight, in the relationship you want to be in or working in your dream job? You are not alone, but what is there about where you are right now that you can make friends with? Can you take a breath and just be thankful for where you are now? How about being grateful you have a vision of where you want to be someday and have faith you will get there? Gratitude can turn around many a situation and it helps us make friends with the present moment.

I play a little game with myself when I'm stuck in traffic or stuck in a long line somewhere. I used to get so frustrated over this. My thought was "I gotta get out of here, this is driving me nuts" and guess what, my thoughts would cause my result and I would be going nuts. Inside I was seething I had to wait in traffic or in a long line. But now, when I find myself in a situation like this, I start to think about what I'm grateful for instead. These are not huge gratitudes, they are very simple ones like "I'm glad my gas tank is full right now" or "I'm so grateful I can crank the tunes in my car and listen to music as I wait". Next time you have to wait in line, feel free to make a mental list of gratitudes, maybe your wait will be more bearable.

CHALLENGE

Try and "make friends with the present moment".

Don't wish a second of your day away.

Make peace with the present moment.

Use the following space to write down your thoughts on this chapter.

chapter forty-seven

GROWTH

"As we begin to grow, we begin to think less of something as being wrong and have more understanding of things being different."

– Deborah Hanlon
In the Presence of Proof

In Chapter 29 I talk about forgiveness and how by letting go, we grow. And this quote is another great reminder of what can happen as we begin to grow. When I first read it, I had to reread it again to fully understand what she was saying; which is growth requires awareness of people and events that surround us.

Get out your mental mat because you are going to need it to answer some questions. Do you have tolerance of others when their views are different from yours? Are you quick to call a situation or a person "wrong" when you don't agree with it or them? Be honest. It seems to me, we often are unaccepting of anyone or anything that is different from the way we think it should be. Does anyone else feel this way? The news gives us daily examples of people who think it's their way or the highway. Social media has allowed everyone in the world a platform to stand up and rant about what they believe is right and how anyone who doesn't agree with them is wrong. If I look back on the past, even 10 years ago, I feel people kept their opinions more to themselves and I'm not sure that was a bad thing. Maybe you disagreed with someone but you didn't use a soap box to stand on and tell the world about it. So many of us are caught up in proving we're right, we don't even stop to listen to someone else or even consider there could be another way of looking at or doing something. We're stuck in the mentality that this is the way it's always been done, the way we were taught, or the way we think is best. Which if you really think about it, is just your opinion about what it is. Why can't someone else have a different opinion and they still be right? I love the statement "can we agree to disagree?" because it's accepting we have differences and it's also respecting those differences. You may remember this statement from Chapter 15. You can go back and refresh your memory if you would like.

But for right now, think about this example. Although I hate politics, I'm using it because there is so much turmoil going on right now in the political arena and we are letting our differences get in the way of our similarities. If you ask most people in the U.S. they would say they love America and they want what is best for America. If you polled 10, 20, even 100 or 1000 people on the street, how many would state, politics aside, they love America? I think almost everyone would. Still, most people have chosen a side in politics and they are 100% certain their side is the right side and the other side is wrong. And not only do we think we are right, we begin to cringe when we hear someone else trying to explain their view. This is because our thoughts create our feelings and our feelings create our actions and reactions. I'm guilty of cringing too and I'm working on it. I try to practice having an open mind and being more tolerant of those with a different point of view. I want to understand their view and where it's coming from. And when I feel myself getting frustrated I take a deep breath and remember it's ok. None of us are wrong, we're all just different.

CHALLENGE

The next time you think someone is wrong,
stop and have more understanding of them
being different. Even if you think they are wrong,
don't tell them so. Maybe respond instead with
"that's an interesting point I never thought of".
Practice being more tolerant and realize
our differences are what make us unique.
We don't have to agree on everything.

Use the space below to take notes or write down some thoughts.

chapter forty-eight

FAILURE IS AN OPTION

"Failure IS an option,
for it is only by learning from our mistakes
that we grow and succeed."

\- Annette Q

We've all heard the famous quote from Apollo 13 "Failure is not an option". A great movie and a phenomenal story of what could truly have been a disaster but instead is a story of persistence and perseverance. Mission Control had to succeed in getting the astronauts home from space; failure was NOT an option. In every day life we are rarely dealing with life and death situations (thank God), although you would think we are by the way we sometimes act when things don't work out the way we want. We have become a society with zero tolerance for failure and often don't try at all for fear of failure.

Do you want to accomplish something, maybe start a business, learn a language or an instrument, but you don't want to go through the challenges you may encounter to achieve it? Do you want to jump to the part where you've mastered it or you're already successful and you don't want to go through any failure to get there? If you are like most people, you want to succeed with the first try because you believe: "failure is not an option".

Now let's stretch our minds a bit and think: what if failure was not only an option but necessary in order for us to get where we want to be? What if we knew ahead we were going to fail, but we were going to learn from each mistake, and eventually succeed? Would you go for it then? Think of all the great inventors and businessmen who did not succeed the first time, who failed so many times and didn't give up and eventually succeeded? Did you know Walt Disney was fired from the Kansas City Star because his editor felt he "lacked imagination and had no good ideas"? Oprah Winfrey was publicly fired from her first television job for getting "too emotionally invested in her stories." Imagine if Oprah said, "I'm not good at this TV thing" and stopped her television career because of this one failure. Did you know Vera Wang failed to make the 1968 US Olympic figure-skating team? She failed at skating and then she became an editor at Vogue, but was passed over for the editor-in-chief position. These two failures helped her become one of the most successful designers of our time. Another failure turned into a success is the story of Harry Potter by J.K. Rowling; it was rejected 12 times by various publishers before one finally accepted it. Twelve rejections, can you imagine? But even after all those rejections she still kept trying to get someone to publish it, and she did, as we all know. Even Thomas Edison and Albert Einstein failed many times before they succeeded.

You see, failure IS an option. The key to failure is you need to learn from your mistakes . You need to determine what you may have done differently, do it and proceed. I talk to many people about their desire to try something new and they will comment something like "yeah, well I tried that once and it didn't work". That's it; they tried once and it didn't work and they stopped trying. This I find very interesting. They (in their mind) failed and stopped trying. It was a "one try and I'm done" mentality. Imagine if the people I previously mentioned had this mindset.

We let our egos get the best of us when we think failure means we're not good enough, or we are less than who we are. Who really cares if you try something and it doesn't work? The answer is mainly YOU. And when I say You, I'm talking about your Ego. So tell your Ego to calm down, it doesn't know everything. It may think it does, but it doesn't.

And what's the big deal if you do fail? Seriously...is it life or death if you succeed or not? Because if it's not, why not try it anyway and if it doesn't work out LEARN from it. Figure out what you may have done differently if you were to try again, and TRY Again. Think of failure as an option that you can welcome because it is going to teach you something, rather than being the worst possible fate you can imagine. You will succeed, but not if you stop trying.

CHALLENGE

The next time something doesn't work out
and you feel you failed, try again.
Your ego may tell you to stop,
in fact your ego will tell you to stop, but don't.
Learn something from it, and try again.
Think of failure as an option—not the opposite.
Remember: "Failure IS an option,
for it is only by learning from our mistakes
that we grow and succeed."

What do you want to try but you are afraid of failing? Use the space below to answer this question and record your thoughts on failure being an option.

chapter forty-nine

TAKING CHANCES

> *"The nervousness felt in taking chances is quickly replaced by the thrill of doing so."*
>
> - Annette Q

This quote is another one I made up and I put it on the Christmas card I referenced in a previous chapter. Get ready to expand your mind as we think about this quote a little further. We've all experienced times when we were afraid to do something. Think back to your childhood, do you recall when your training wheels came off your bike? I remember thinking once these wheels are off I'm going to fall right off this bike; it's going to topple to one side, how can it stand up with just two wheels? I can still picture my brother Stan running beside me, holding onto the back of my seat to keep me from falling and then voila, he let go! I was scared but it changed to exhilaration fast. The thrill of riding on two wheels all by myself took over all the fears I had.

We usually are elated after we take a chance on something. But for some reason, we don't recall those moments when we are faced with another fearful challenge. The "thrill of doing" is forgotten. But we can recover our nerves. How? By stretching our minds a bit more.

What are you nervous to do right now? Is there something in your life you've been thinking about doing but fear has paralyzed your mind and your will? Our thoughts determine our feelings. If you are feeling hesitant or threatened, it's because your mind is telling you all the horrible things that may happen or go wrong. Our nerves take over because we begin to think crazy thoughts. We play a number of doomsday scenarios in our head. We tell ourselves if we take this opportunity, if we take this chance, the outcome is not going to be good. "Play it Safe" our mind tells us. Our mind wants to be efficient, it does not want to challenge itself. It wants you to take the path of least resistance. The path of least resistance is always safe. It's your comfort zone. It's where we feel the most comfortable. I like to say your comfort zone would like you to leave. You've overstayed your welcome.

Now I want you to recall a time or two when you were afraid to do something but you did it anyway. I bet you were glad you did. I bet you were even excited after you did and couldn't wait to tell someone. As you think about it, notice how you feel. Are you smiling as you remember it? You can also remember this the next time you want to do something and you start to get nervous about it. Remember that feeling and remember "The nervousness felt in taking chances is quickly replaced by the thrill of doing so."

CHALLENGE

Pick one thing you are nervous about doing and do it anyway. Instead of letting your mind go through negative scenarios of what's going to happen, do the opposite. Think a thought as simple as

"all will be well". When a negative thought
creeps in your mind, notice it but then release it.
If you want to add a little more fun,
what does that negative thought look like?
Give it life for a second and make it into a living object.
Maybe it's an animal, maybe it's a cartoon character
or fictitious person. Once you have
your own description of it, literally picture yourself
walking it out the door just like you're going
to walk it out of your mind.

Use the following space to write down your thoughts on this chapter.

chapter fifty

SAY YES TO YOU

"You can't say yes to everything
and not say yes to taking care of yourself.
To not say yes to health."

– Shonda Rhimes

Taking care of our mental and physical health is our responsibility. No one can do it for us. Science has proven how important it is to stay in physical shape. Now more than ever, they are discovering the benefits of a healthy mind and the correlation between a healthy mind and the ability to deal with stress. Knowing this, what is your real reason for not saying YES to your health? Are you afraid to take the first step, or do you not know how to take the first step? I want you to really try and think about why you are not a priority in your own life. Some people think if they make themselves a priority that's being selfish. It's not. Another quote I love and have used before as one of my daily quotes is "You do not have to set yourself on fire to keep others warm". Think about that for a moment. You don't have to sacrifice your health in order to keep others healthy. If you really want to take care of others, you need to take care of your health. If we get sick from not taking care of ourselves, we will be no good to others so it is our responsibility to take care of ourselves. Our health is not just important to us, it's important to them too. The healthier we are both physically and mentally the happier we will be. And when we are happier, we tend to respond to people and deal with people in a much better way.

Shonda's words made me think about all the people pleasers out there. Do you belong to this group and how do you know if you are? Here's some signs that can help you identify if you are a people pleaser: you find it hard to say no to others; every second of your day is filled with something you have to do for someone else; you may complain a little, but deep down you feel a sense of pride in being able to do it all for others.

If you are a people pleaser stop ignoring yourself and start taking care of YOU. Stop repeating the same excuses; you don't have the time; your life is crazy busy; you have to take care of your kids, your husband, your parents, a friend who needs you. You say you'll take care of your needs after everyone else is taken care. It's a very noble thought. And you are a very kind person for thinking this way. But I now want you to stretch your mind a bit and think about how long have you been saying this to yourself? Have you been saying it just for a week, or has it been a month, or has it been years? The list of people you need to take care of keeps piling up, the list of things you feel you need to do before you take care of yourself keeps piling up too. Stop putting yourself and your health on the back burner. You are sacrificing your health for everyone else's. It's time to say Yes to You!

CHALLENGE

Think about why you say yes to everyone but yourself.
Write down your thoughts on this.
Writing down your thoughts on anything
is such a great healing tool. We learn so much
about ourselves when we write what is on our mind.
Start making your health a priority.

Use the space below to take notes or write down some thoughts.

chapter fifty-one

BE YOU

"Be you, the world will adjust."

- Author Unknown

This quote is simple, succinct and so wise. Think carefully before you answer these questions and be honest with yourself when answering them. How often do you adjust for others? How often do you do something even if you don't want to, because either you want someone to think well of you or you do it for the opposite reason...because you fear what they will think of you if you don't? Are you a people pleaser? If you are, you are not alone; there's a lot of us out there. We're taught at a young age to be nice to others-which we should, but there is a difference between being nice to others and losing yourself in the process. Kindness is never overrated. We should always be kind. What I want you to think about is—are you being true to yourself? Or, are you always putting others before yourself? Do you fill your time with doing everything for everyone else and leave no time for YOU?

I want you to stretch your mind and think about this question: if you aren't being true to you, why is that ok? How can that be admirable? Being our authentic self is the best thing we can give ourselves and those around us. We all know people who are phony, and we don't tend to like them. So just "Be you, the world will adjust!"

Perhaps we often are not true to ourselves because we feel we will disappoint others. We've already in our mind thought someone is going to be upset if we don't do what they ask or follow their plans for us. And so we begrudgingly take on tasks or go along with plans which we really want nothing to do with in the first place. We overcommit to others and we make no commitment to ourselves. We, in essence, lose our true selves when we are too busy pleasing others. We hold the power for us, yet we give our power away too often when we overcommit to others and let their needs come before ours.

How can we start to take back our power? Awareness is always the first step in changing any behavior. Try this: The next time you find yourself in a situation where you know what you want to do but the little voice in your head starts telling you what others may want you to do, notice the voice of conflict first, this is important. Then, after you notice it, be true to yourself in your response. If you want to say no, say no kindly. You could respond "I'm sorry that doesn't work for me". And please, don't explain why. It's not necessary.

You don't need to come up with an excuse why, just say it doesn't work for you. People will not question you if you respond this way. When we explain our excuse, it makes people think you really want to attend the event you just said no to, and often the person who asked us starts coming up with a solution for us. They might suggest "well maybe you can come later"; or "maybe you can change your plans." They think you do want to go and they try to come up with a way you can make it happen. Guess what the real truth is though, it's if you say no they will adjust. Maybe they'll be hurt or maybe they'll be mad, but they will survive and so will the relationship.

CHALLENGE

Just be YOU.
The challenge is not learning to say no
to things you don't want to do,
it's realizing you can be who you are.
Whether you say yes or no,
you should make decisions based on who you are
and what you want to do,
not what you think others want you to do.
"Be you, the world will adjust."

Use the following space to write down your thoughts on this chapter.

chapter fifty-two

BETTER THAN I USED TO BE

> *"I ain't as good as I'm gonna get, but I'm better than I used to be."*
>
> – Song performed by Tim McGraw
> (written by: Bryan Simpson/Ashley Gorley)

This chapter is about recognizing our growth. As we start to become more aware of our thoughts, we begin to realize that they are the source of our feelings, which in turn determine our actions which lead to our results. Our actions may or may not be harmful to us and other people we encounter. I'm going to continue with some of the lyrics in the first verse of the song because it will help us with our mind yoga:

> I know how to hold a grudge,
> I can send a bridge up in smoke
> And I can't count the people I've let down,
> the hearts I broke
> You ain't gotta dig too deep if you want to
> find some dirt on me
> But I'm learning who you've been
> Ain't who you've got to be

The rest of the lyrics are printed at the end of this chapter.

So let's stretch our minds. Have you ever held a grudge? Have you blown up at anyone? I'm sure we all have let down people and not even have known it. Every line in this verse most of us have been guilty of at some point in our life. How about "You ain't gotta dig too deep if you want to find some dirt on me"? You know lucky for some of us the internet wasn't around when we were younger. I think we all can agree there are some moments in our life we are not proud of and we'd prefer for them to be forgotten and not dredged up and remembered.

Since you are reading this book I do know you are a person who is interested in improvement. You are a person who is open to hearing another point of view. You are someone who wants to gain control over your thoughts and actions, not let life lead you in any direction the wind may blow. And I commend you for that, for joining me in some mind stretching exercises, for trying to apply this information and techniques to find more peace. And for these reasons I ask you to get out your mental mat and answer the question: Are you a better person now than you used to be? As we get older we often talk about our past, and it's fun to recall old memories that brought us joy and still do when we revisit them in our minds. I love looking at old photo albums (remember them?) and recalling the memory of the photograph, the people I was with, the place we were at, something funny that happened the day the photo was taken.

But, I also know I'm a better person now than I was then. How do I know this? Because I'm much more aware now of who I am and I'm more conscious of how I treat others. I now try to respond rather than react to situations. Do I forget sometimes and fall back into old ways, sure I do. But, I now take full responsibility for my thoughts, feelings and actions. I'm a much more open minded person. I want to continue to learn new things as I age and I want to know more about others. Having said this, do I get mad, angry, sad or down on myself or others—absolutely.

I'm human and because of that, I'm never going to be perfect and I'm never going to have bliss 100% of the time. And I'm ok with that. How come? Well, to paraphrase another part of the song: "I'm learning who I've been isn't who I have to be."

So what about you? Do you believe people can change? Do you believe who you've been is who you have to be, or it isn't who you have to be? Last summer I was in a discussion with a friend who told me she believes that after a certain age people can't change. I couldn't disagree more. Anyone can change, they just have to want to change and they have to work at doing so. It's not a process that happens overnight, it takes time and effort. But it can happen. And that's how I know:

> "I ain't as good as I'm gonna get
> But I'm better than I used to be"

CHALLENGE :

Decide if you want to be a better version of yourself
and really think about how you can do that.
What will you do differently?
It could be as simple as listening more to others
or spending more time with those you care about.
It doesn't matter what,
it's just awesome you're recognizing
you want to be better than you used to be.

Use the space below to start writing your vision for the best version of yourself and how you are going to achieve becoming this person.

Lyrics to Better Than I Used To Be

Written by: Bryan Simpson and Ashley Gorley

www.lyrics.com - May 16, 2019

I know how to hold a grudge
I can send a bridge up in smoke
And I can't count the people I've let down,
the hearts I've broke
You ain't gotta dig too deep
If you wanna find some dirt on me
But I'm learning who you've been
Ain't who you've got to be
It's gonna be an uphill climb
Aww honey I won't lie

I ain't no angel
I still got a few more dances with the devil
I'm cleanin up my act, little by little
I'm getting there
I can finally stand the man in the mirror I see
I ain't as good as I'm gonna get
But I'm better than I used to be

I've pinned a lot of demons to the ground
I've got a few old habits left
There's one or two I might need you to help me get
Standin in the rain so long has left me with a little rust
But put some faith in me
And someday you'll see
There's a diamond under all this dust

I ain't no angel
I still got a few more dances with the devil
I'm cleanin up my act, little by little
I'm getting there
I can finally stand the man in the mirror I see
I ain't as good as I'm gonna get
But I'm better than I used to be

acknowledgements

There are many people
to whom I am grateful
for making this book possible.

To my husband Arch, I appreciate your acceptance of who I am, your faith in me and your love. I am truly blessed to be married to someone who makes me laugh on a daily basis and who consistently thrives to be a better person. Thank you for being my sounding board, my confidant and my best friend.

To my Mom, and my siblings Jan, Rick, Linda and Dauryne; I thank you all for the love and guidance you have given me through the years. They say you can't pick your family but I would pick each of you to be in my life and am grateful God placed me in our family.

To my closest friends whose quotes I have used on my podcast and in this book; Judy Pawlick, Karen Keis, Karen Macri and the rest of the "GNO" Girls; Laurie Grego, Nancy Zieker, Laura Hinman, Kim Hinman, and Kris Kuznia. Your friendship through the years continues to be one of the most precious gifts I have in my life. I am beyond lucky to have not only grown up with you, but am now privileged to be growing into a better version of myself with you. Just as the commercial from our youth exclaimed; we're not getting older, we're getting better!

To Chuck Ranney, who helped build my "Abundance Room". Although you openly admit you did not agree with my vision, thank you for putting up with my crazy ideas and knowing when it's best for a man to just reply "yes, ma'm" instead of trying to get me to change my mind.

To Deborah Hanlon who told me to "keep writing" and for all the other words of wisdom you have provided to me over the last few years. Thank you for helping me understand patience can be peaceful and for your spiritual guidance.

To my cousin June Goggi who edited this book for me. I appreciate your time, your editing skills, the gift you sent with reference to Aunt Peg, and your sense of humor which kept me sane during the process. I love every suggestion you made. Thank you for helping me make this dream a reality.

To Michelle Bourque for the tens of thousands of miles we've travelled together, (in separate cars and going to different locations) and for the countless talks and laughs we've had along our separate but similar journeys. The fun is just beginning!

To the Apple Store Employees at Crossgates Mall: I appreciate all your knowledge and everyone's patience as I learned how to record and edit my podcast. Rick, Gary, Colin, and all the others who have helped me— You all Rock!

To Martha Beck for the Life Coach training and Certification program you put together; the tools I learned to help me and others I will forever be grateful for and will use for the rest of my life.

To Brooke Castillo for her wisdom and her further development of the Self Coaching Model. Thank you for being an example of all that is possible.

To Jessika Hazelton at The Troy Book Makers: Thank you for your patience and your professionalism. It has been a pleasure working with you.

And lastly to my Dad, Richard Valenti, who passed away before this book came to fruition. I am beyond grateful for all the love and support you provided me. I cannot even begin to express how much you are missed each and every day.

room to reflect